HENRIK IBSEN
Plays and Problems

Henrik Ibsen.

HENRIK IBSEN

Plays and Problems

BY OTTO HELLER

Professor of the German Language and Literature in
Washington University; Author of "Studies
in Modern German Literature"

BOSTON AND NEW YORK
HOUGHTON MIFFLIN COMPANY
The Riverside Press Cambridge
1912

" Je ne propose rien, je n' impose rien, j' expose."—Joseph Dunoyer.

PREFACE

THE motto of this book, which has been adopted from
Werner Sombart's brilliant work on *Socialism*, is meant
to indicate at one and the same time the purpose of the
great writer to whom it is devoted and, *si parva componere
magnis licet*, the author's own unpresumptuous aim.
The literature that has gathered round the name of
Ibsen is doubtless deemed by many people to be more
than sufficiently copious; and, taken as a whole, it
represents a very respectable level of critical ability.
Nevertheless, a new attempt at interpreting Ibsen for
the English reader can probably justify itself. In the
first place, by the poet's steadily increasing popularity
and his growing importance as a factor of dramatic
progress. In the second, by its obvious difference from
similar treatises in the general point of view, a difference
which naturally leads to a somewhat revised estimate of
the various groups of dramas as regards their artistic and
ethical importance. Whereas in practically all the other
English books on the subject the *romantic* and *historical*
plays are ranked highest and are given a correspondingly
greater amount of space and attention, the present study
is avowedly devoted more particularly to the *social* or
problem plays, and that because of the author's conviction that these plays are more closely connected with our
own private and social concerns. The Selected List of
writings appended to the book enables the reader to sup-

plement from other sources his information about such parts and aspects of Ibsen's work as are not discussed here with sufficient fullness to answer his purpose.

It has been the author's endeavor to acknowledge his specific obligations to other writers. It will be noticed that, both in the text and in the notes, he has drawn quite freely upon the standard English translation of Ibsen, the *Collected Works*, edited by William Archer. From this edition most of the illustrative passages are derived; likewise, the admirable introductions to the several volumes have yielded a large quantity of helpful material. The availability of such excellent translations and, besides, of handy editions of Ibsen's letters, speeches, and jottings, has made it possible to base this presentation step by step upon authentic documents and to ascertain the philosophical significance of views expressed by the characters in action by means of their incessant comparison with the poet's own confidential expressions of opinion. In reading this or any other book on Ibsen the serious student would do well to keep the *Works, Correspondence, Speeches and New Letters,* and the "literary remains" constantly by his side.

The author has, from practical considerations, followed Mr. Archer's method of transliterating the Norwegian names and titles. This has been done at the risk of sacrificing entire consistency. For this reason and because of the somewhat problematical state of spelling in Dano-Norwegian itself, a word will occasionally appear in a twofold orthographical form, as indeed it does within one and the same original edition.

It is hoped that the full index may materially enhance

the usefulness of this study as a book of reference. The Selected List of writings recognizes under one of its subheadings the unique importance of Ibsen for the progress of the woman cause.

Acknowledgments are due to Dr. Lee M. Hollander, of the University of Wisconsin, and Professor George T. Flom, of the University of Illinois, for the contribution of several helpful data. The Index was prepared by Mrs. W. R. Mackenzie. During the printing of this book the author has had the invaluable assistance of his wife.

OTTO HELLER.

WASHINGTON UNIVERSITY,
ST. LOUIS, June, 1912.

CONTENTS

EXPLANATION OF THE NOTES

THE principal abbreviations used in the references to Ibsen's writings are: —

M = Henrik Ibsen. Samlede Vaerker. Mindeudgave. Kristiania og Köbenhavn: Gyldendalske Boghandel. Nordisk Forlag. 1906–07.

CW = The Collected Works of Henrik Ibsen. Copyright edition. New York: Charles Scribner's Sons. 1908. (11 volumes; vol. XII, added in 1911, contains Notes, Scenarios, and Drafts of the Modern Plays.)

SW = Henrik Ibsens Sämtliche Werke in deutscher Sprache. Durchgesehen und eingeleitet von Georg Brandes, Julius Elias, Paul Schlenther. Vom Dichter autorisiert. Berlin: S. Fischer, Verlag.

*SW*ᴵᴵ = the continuation (Zweite Reihe) of *SW*. Nachgelassene Schriften in vier Bänden. Herausgegeben von Julius Elias und Halvdan Koht. Berlin: S. Fischer, Verlag. 1909 (used here in preference over vol. XII of *CW*, because of its greater completeness; and in preference over the *Efterladte Skrifter* on account of the unfamiliarity of most readers with the language of the original).

C = The Correspondence of Henrik Ibsen. The translation edited by Mary Morison. London: Hodder and Stoughton. 1905. Identical with: Letters of Henrik Ibsen. Translated by John Nilsen Laurvik and Mary Morison New York: Duffield and Company. 1908.

SNL = Speeches and New Letters [of] Henrik Ibsen. Translated by Arne Kildal. With an Introduction by Lee M. Hollander and a Bibliographical Appendix. Boston: Richard G. Badger. 1910.

References indicated by superior *numbers* are to Ibsen's writings, including his letters, speeches, etc., and generally, to material contained in the above publications; these references are placed at the foot of the page. Superior *letters* refer to notes at the end of the book. Notes referring to special parts of the plays, and also, as a rule, the quotations in English, are made on the basis of *CW*; in these, only volumes and pages are indicated, unless there is special need of repeating the title. Hence, for example, vol. II, p. 300, would stand for *CW*, vol. II, p. 300.

INTRODUCTION

THE aim of showing the importance of Henrik Ibsen, both as a poet and a moral teacher, suggests at the outset a definite and emphatic assertion that he was a highly potent factor in modern life in both these spiritual functions. A score of years ago Ibsen was still universally the object of embittered contests and argument. But now he is already an historic personage and his great cultural significance is acknowledged in all parts of the civilized world. In this country the recognition of the great Scandinavian has been slower than elsewhere; but now here also a change from the reluctant attitude towards him is making itself rapidly felt.

The reason for this tardiness in the acceptance of one of the greatest men of modern times may be worth pointing out. It is due to our luckless democratic way of looking at all things through the childish eyes of the majority, the same habit to which we owe our national deprecation of art and our backwardness in so many phases of intellectual life.

What does the "compact majority" expect of its intellectual leaders and masters? Merely that they conform to its ruling tastes and desires. And so reasonable at first blush seems this demand, as to make us seriously doubt whether a writer may safely be counted among the great unless his thought and art are in harmony with at least a fairly representative number of his contemporaries. If anything like a law could be claimed to have governed the evolution of art, it would in all likelihood be this, that, throughout the so-called golden ages, artists, with few exceptions, have in a rational degree subserved the preferences of their public. Of none of the arts may this be stated with fuller truth than of the drama. The Greek tragedy, with its slow-wound action, stately tirades, and long-breathed choral harangues, was fashioned to the taste of a people fond of philosophic expatiation, addicted to dignified leisure, accustomed to manage their life to the order of a pronounced æsthetic bias. So Shakespeare's drama, in its nervous, not infrequently jerky movement, its ornate phraseology, its vivid spectacular situations, was admirably adapted to the pompous style of England during the later Renaissance, to audiences made up of courtiers and burgesses, armigerous both of them and amply inured to the tumults and atrocities of militant politics. Molière wrought for a public basking in the effulgence of the *Roi Soleil*, quick-witted, dignifiedly gay in external demeanor, and rather more refined in speech than sentiment. Their keen sense of humor, still plentifully lacking in delicacy, loved to be tickled by base ribaldry, yet was finical enough to make acknowledgment with smiles, not guffaws.

Such is the ancestry of modern German drama, and so long as German dramatists rested content with the approbation of the upper castes or of the "intellectuals," the national sense, which as a rule resides rather in the plain people, was largely left unsatisfied. For aristocracy of any sort tends to an international, cosmopolitan form of culture. Even of Goethe, anchored though he was with his deepest roots in the ground of his nationality, it is true on the whole that he made his appeal to the "elect," not to the "people." Schiller was the first to ring a change on this state of things by addressing himself courageously to the entire population of his country in all its social strata at one time. He was the great popularizer of our theatre, and remained for almost a century the guiding spirit of the German drama of which Schiller's matchless tragedies are still by many people regarded as the surpassing manifestoes. Schiller's position, while it demonstrates a whole people's gratitude to those who respond to its desires, does not however furnish a weapon of self-defense to the "popularizers" of drama, or rather its diluters. Schiller's case rather proves that the power of popular influence wrought upon a poet may be vastly inferior to the strength that radiates from his own personality. Indeed, whereas the secret of ephemeral power is only too often found in paltriness or mediocrity, an influence of enduring force such as Schiller exerts on the Germans can only emanate from a strong and self-assertive character. No poet lives beyond his day who does not exceed the average in mental stature, or who, through a selfish sense of fear of the "general," allows himself to be ground down to the conventional size and shape. Schiller, no less than Ibsen, forced his moral demands tyrannically upon his contemporaries. And in the long run your moral despot, provided he be high-minded, vigorous, and able, has a better chance of fame than the pliant time-server. However, there is a great difference between the two cases. For quite apart from the striking dissimilarities between the poets themselves, the public, through the gradual growth of social organization, has become greatly altered.

The modern dramatist, unless his lines are unhappily cast in the unpromising soil of the so-called Anglo-Saxon civilizations, where the only emotion which plays a part in the drama is that of love, deals with a public much less homogeneous in tastes and opinions than that of Schiller or Goethe, not to speak of Shakespeare and the ancients. His is a public with many minds, or, what comes to the same thing, a public with a wistfully troubled spirit and a mind not yet made up. Where our ancestors were so restfully sure about things, we are uncertain and skeptical pending the arrival of fresh bulletins from science. We have become aroused to many a subject to which the "good old times" gave scarcely a perturbing thought. We are breaking into the consciousness of strange new meanings in life and nature. As a result, the excuse for a uniform standard of art has disappeared along with a ubiquitous code of moral opinion for the drama of continental Europe; whether temporarily or permanently, cannot be settled here.

The enlightened modern public, then, makes to a moralizing dramatist this all-important concession that there need be no absolute and only way of facing the world. Nor are things always as they seem. A thing that seems astoundingly complicated to one person may strike another as extremely simple, or — more frequently — what appears quite simple to some may impress others as being defiantly intricate. Being independents and skeptics, we grant the poet the same privileges which we arrogate to ourselves, the right of holding personal views and original intentions; but we are not unthinking skeptics, hence we do not care to have him publish his views abroad unless they are convincing, or at least enlightening and stimulating. With pedants, smatterers, and dabblers we are out of patience, whereas a forceful though never so heterodox personality finds a wider echo and a readier following in the intellectual centres of Europe to-day than was the case at any former period. Thus the worship of heroes has by no means died with our faith in authority. The world still recognizes that it cannot dispense with leaders. Yet there is a difference, according to various states of civilization. For instance, a crudely organized democracy will unhesitatingly reject leaders who, in regard to the major policies of public and private life, are not in accord with the mind of the mass or do not diplomatically pretend to be. Its "great" men are great only in the measure in which they catch and seemingly reflect the spirit of the throng. For example, if it is given to a man by virtue of his station and personal blandishments to emphasize and reinforce the people's natural impulse for civic righteousness, this most elementary manifestation of good will and courage will be enough to magnify to the size of a hero a brave, well-meaning citizen, though intellectually he be never so commonplace. We may well speculate, in the light of this fact, on the popular apotheosis of such "good average" men as William Jennings Bryan or Theodore Roosevelt.

The European order of society, for all its external restraints, makes larger allowances than does the American order for the individualist and iconoclast, for the multifarious varieties of the *studens rerum novarum*, whose efforts somehow, in spite of conflicts and clashes, converge towards higher common ideals.[a] Consequently that man in whose work the differentiating tendencies of the time are most completely embodied and exposed is bound sooner or later to come into his own, if a unique artistic power seconds his moral purpose. Ibsen was one of the comparatively rare writers who form an independent estimate of moral views and personal problems by their own light instead of reflecting in a pleasing mirror the "general view," which almost of necessity must be fallacious and obsolete.[b] In this or that respect he was unquestionably outranked by many of his contemporaries in Germany, France, Russia, Italy, and Belgium, but what other writer of the nineteenth century has become to the same extent a European influence? While still living, his historic importance was recognized, as the chief expositor of ideas which specifically distinguish our age from the past, and as the discoverer of a new vehicle for their expression. In this typical character he is to be discussed in the following pages; and that *sine ira et studio;* since Ibsen's cause still requires to be brought fairly before the popular opinion of the English-speaking public, we must be scrupulously careful to distinguish between Ibsen the moralist and Ibsen the poet, between the subjective and the objective aspect of his utterance, that is to say, between opinions which he personally advocates and the characteristic views of his *dramatis personæ.*

It is to a lack of this just discrimination that the delay of Ibsen's ascendancy among us is chiefly due. The perplexing effect of such a writer on a public habituated to

the moods, manners, and morals of the Anglo-Saxon
stage-land is viewed by a recent witty writer as altogether natural. Theirs was not an attitude of hostility
against the Norwegian playwright, but merely the revolt
of conservatism against what is unfamiliar and the pro-
test of playful optimism against the perversion of the
drama to serious purposes. Such is the judicious opinion
of Mr. Frank Moore Colby, who goes on to say: "No
doubt the excellent gentlemen who were the most vitu-
perative in the capacity as critics were the most enrap-
tured as playgoers. For a gift like Ibsen's enlivens these
jaded folk more than they are willing to admit. Deeply
absorbed at the time in the doings of the disagreeable
characters, they afterward define their sensation as one
of loathing, and they include the playwright in their
pious hatred, like newsboys at a melodrama pelting the
man in the villain's part. It comes from the national habit
of making optimism actually a matter of conscience, and
denying the validity of any feeling unless it is a sleepy
one. Now, of course, if a man's own wits are precisely on
the level of the modern American and English stage,
there can be no quarrel with him for disliking Ibsen. If
there is no lurking discontent with our stage and its
traditions, and with the very best plays of Anglo-Saxon
origin produced in this country during the last twenty
years, an Ibsen play will surely seem a malicious interruption. What in the world has a good, placid American
audience to do with this half-mad old Scandinavian?
He writes only for those who go to the theatre to be
disturbed." [c]

The cause of our playgoers' indignant dissatisfaction

with Henrik Ibsen is simply the terrible moral earnestness of the man. He feels that certain things which the compact majority has silently conspired to keep quiet should be said, therefore he proceeds to say them. Dr. Stockmann, the "Enemy of the People," represents best among his figures the author's frame of mind. When this doctor discovers that the reputed health resort over which he presides is in reality a pest-hole, he will not join in the proposed conspiracy of silence, but firmly, in loud voice, declares the truth, knowing full well that his utterance must cost him his place and living. This is precisely the case of Ibsen. What is it that makes such cases so exceptional if not the universality of rank cowardice and hypocrisy in large ranks of "good" society? Out of ordinary respect for human intelligence we must credit with an ability to tell the wrong and the evil an enormous number of persons who never, on any account, open their mouths against it. It is due to human nature to concede further that very many people are even aroused, by their fellow creatures' turpidity, to contempt and righteous wrath, yet even they, as a rule, refrain from speaking out. When pressed for reasons, these good people are apt to confess their aversion to polemics, — or they meekly decline to "pose as reformers," and with a tolerant smile inform the impatient advocate of probity that there does not seem much use in fighting against "human nature."

They hold the Panglossian view, — that this is the best of all possible worlds, — and have made up their practical minds to make the best of it. They believe in making the best of things that are bad and always will be bad. And because of this unwreckable faith in the bad-ness of things, such people are known as — optimists. The determination to speak out the truth, observable in Ibsen as well as in many of his compatriots, is rather characteristic of countries where literature is young and unhackneyed, so that many things have a chance of being said for the first time, coming with warmth, vigor, and virgin freshness straight from the heart. Since out of the mouths of babes and sucklings has been ordained strength, we may in these days look without amazement upon the spectacle of great and mighty nations seeking increase in art and wisdom from the weaker and more undeveloped. Learned Germany and cultured France have been going to school to little Norway and barbaric Russia. My excuse for offering this new study of Henrik Ibsen to the English-speaking public is grounded in a conviction that England and the United States are also becoming "Ibsenreif," ready to listen to the message of the greatest dramatic poet of our age, and one of its foremost social preachers.

HENRIK IBSEN
PLAYS AND PROBLEMS

CHAPTER I

IBSEN THE SCANDINAVIAN

THAT great Danish scholar, George Brandes, has commiserated Henrik Ibsen — and, by indirection, himself, — for belonging to a minor nationality. Certainly the herculean task of converting the world to his views is rendered all the more difficult for a writer when but few can comprehend his medium of communication. There may, however, be pointed out some compensations for the disadvantage. In a small country, as a rule, the national pride and national sense are strongly developed. The population of such a country is apt to be more homogeneous in its character, and for this reason it is sometimes easier for a masterful intellect to assert its claim to leadership. Besides, Ibsen addressed himself from the beginning to a larger audience than that of Norway. As a believer in Scandinavian union he used in his works the Dano-Norwegian literary speech — as did Björnson, Lie, Kielland, Hamsun, and many others. At the time when Norway cut itself loose from Denmark (1814) there was no great difference between the two languages; since then they have been growing steadily apart. A movement for the reconstruction of a separate Norse language, based on the surviving peasant dialects, took its origin from the poet Henrik Wergeland's campaign, to which some reference will presently be made. An increasingly successful agitation for this artificial national language, named *Landsmaal*, has been carried on for upward of half a century, and the movement in its favor, under the name of *Maalstraev*, is still making headway.[a] Ibsen, though he made free use of Norwegian idioms in this *Schriftsprache*, at no time aligned himself on the side of the linguistic reformers.

Our initial consideration is due to the homeland of our poet. Norway, being practically the Ultima Thule of Western civilization and by her insular remoteness prevented from direct contact with central European culture, has had, till recent times, but a loose connection with the literary life of Europe, and has been slower even than her sister nations of Sweden and Denmark to claim a fair place among the culture-producing nations of the earth. The delay was not due to any lack of a national sense for letters. In the very remote past Norsemen took their part vigorously enough in laying the foundations of an imperishable world literature. By their faithful guardianship over a rich treasure of sagas both native and imported, by their proficiency in creating and transmuting the raw material of poetry, the world's store of artistic grandeur and romance has enormously profited. But about the middle period of its history Norway as a radiator of literary culture went, almost suddenly, into a long eclipse. Having lost her autonomy she was reduced, from 1397 till 1814, to a virtual dependency of the Danish Crown. This long period was marked by such a lethargy

of the spiritual activities that it is quite fittingly termed
"the night of four centuries." Even the enlightening
eighteenth century brought Norway hardly the faintest
shimmer of a dawning day. It would not have been surprising had the last promise of a better future automat-
ically perished in this total darkness. When at last Norway issued from her deathlike stupor, it required no deep
sagacity to fathom the causes of her salvation. The rich
racial strain of modern Norse literature is by no means
accidental. It is a heritage preserved by the quiet, steady
upkeeping of folk poetry throughout that almost inter-
minable age of depression. By virtue of this basic condi-
tion for a literary revival of national scope, some very
difficult obstacles were quickly overcome, and Scandinavian literature was able to build up in a short space of
time such a tremendous international influence as to
surpass the highest hopes of the patriots.

In 1814 Norway reclaimed her lost independence. On
May 17th of that year — the day is observed as the chief
national holiday — she detached herself permanently
from Denmark, formulated her own organic statutes, and
joined with Sweden on equal terms in a new dual mon-
archy. But the birthday of the new literature fell much
later. The nineteenth century was more than half gone
before Norway ceased to be a negligible factor in the culture of Europe. The same is true, however, of Scandinavia as a whole. Her books were sealed to the English-
speaking world by reason of their unfamiliar language,
and her fame rested mainly on the achievements of her
great discoverers, scientists, and artists: Tycho Brahe,
Linnæus, Berzelius, Thorwaldsen. Of her writers, Holberg,

Tegnér, and Andersen were about the only ones that were fairly appreciated.

In Norway from about 1830 a new literature was forming along two divergent lines of development. It will tend to the better comprehension of Ibsen's earlier works to indicate these lines by pointing to the feud between the two factions of which Henrik Wergeland (1808–1845) and Johan Sebastian Welhaven (1807–1873) were the acknowledged leaders. Wergeland's literary activity stood for nationalism, i.e., for the cultivation of specifically Norwegian traits. Although a theologian by education, Wergeland was a radical of decidedly revolutionary proclivities, a rationalist and adherent of eighteenth century deism. He was the author of odes and songs and a lyric-dramatic poem, entitled *Skabelsen, Mennesket og Messias* ("Creation, Man, and the Messiah"), highly rhetorical products without a fine sense of form. The conflict between him and the symbolist Welhaven was not caused only by æsthetic antagonism; rather, fundamentally, by the question in which of the two directions Norwegian culture was to be furthered. Welhaven was the leader of the so-called "Intellectuals." His party took the ground that the culture of Norway should develop from the premises that existed; its present state of culture had been evolved in the union with Denmark, and it would be more than folly to sacrifice, beside much further gain from the same source, the connection with general European culture which the union with Denmark had opened up. In a beautiful set of sonnets, *Norges Damring* (1834), he scouted the onesidedness of the "patriots," contending that intellectual life cannot be made to spring from nothing. But this set of poems was received by the opposition as a traitorous manifesto. One of Welhaven's nearest spiritual kinsmen was Andreas Munch (1811–1884). Undeniably, Ibsen was very strongly influenced by these tendencies.

Certainly the "Ultra-Norwegianists" were then still lacking a sound basis for their separatistic endeavors. At any rate, a beginning was made about that time in laying a proper foundation for a national literature. Peter Christian Asbjörnsen (1812–1885), a forester by profession, and Bishop Jörgen Moe (1813–1882) performed for their country the same service that the brothers Grimm performed for Germany. By their intelligent perseverance a great wealth of ancient tales and sagas was conserved without a perceptible loss of their popular tone and flavor. Asbjörnsen's *Norske Huldre-eventyr og Folkesagn* became for Ibsen's early poetry a source and influence of invaluable importance; the same was undoubtedly true of other collections inspired by these two pioneers. Foremost to be named among such collectors of songs and folklore are Magnus Brostrup Landstad (1802–1880) and Sophus Elseus Bugge (1833–1867).

The progress of the literary revival was at first rather slow. Here again the same is true of Scandinavia as a whole. For our own era Sören Aaby Kierkegaard (1813–1855), Denmark's greatest thinker, was the first Scandinavian of some European importance. What enormous advance comes forcibly to one's mind as one thinks of the many Scandinavian names that must be included among the principal writers of the present! Beside Ibsen and Björnson there suggest themselves at once spontaneously the names of Selma Lagerlöf, Jonas Lie, J. P. Jacobsen, Alexander Strindberg, George and Edvard Brandes, Alexander Kielland, Arne Garborg, Hermann Bang, Knut Hamsun, and a host of others. It goes without saying that this memorable rise of the æsthetic faculties was coextensive with a general intellectual, social, and political growth.[b] So far as regards Norway in particular, her reconstitution as a separate wholly autonomous commonwealth under a self-chosen dynasty (1905), after an almost century-old union with Sweden, bespeaks irrefutably the vitality of her long-harbored political aspirations. Equally, the final world-wide recognition of Henrik Ibsen, being simultaneous with the national ascendancy, betokens the little country's valid claim to international prestige in the realm of thought and art.

Out of their "night of four centuries," then, the Norwegians have apparently arisen a wide-awake people, well rested for the upbuilding work of the day. They are seen to display a sort of unfagged vigor in coping with the problems peculiar to our era. Ibsen applies to them, though in a derogatory sense, the sobriquet "Yankees of the Old World," and the name fits them more closely certainly than it fits the inhabitants of Prussia or even of Holland, on whom one hears it occasionally bestowed. For in Norway the free processes of opinion are not so much embarrassed as in those other lands by the force of memories; the break-up of traditions is not so much inhibited by a sense of piety. Hence the people's surprising readiness to readjust by radical changes their social and civic machinery, as when early in the past century the titles and privileges of noble birth were at one stroke abolished. In one of the greatest issues of democracy, Norway has led the van by her consistent course of extending the civic rights and liberties of the citizen and providing for a direct mode of all national and territorial elections. Norway has also been foremost to improve the civic status of woman, both before the civil law and through the enactment of female franchise. By the new statutes women take part in municipal elections under the same conditions of franchise as men. They are entitled to a direct vote from the age of twenty-five; in order to exercise her franchise a woman must only be paying an income tax on the trifling annual income of three hundred (in the larger cities four hundred) kroner, which, however, her husband may pay in her name if they have property in common.

The Norwegians prove themselves in many other directions an energetic and progressive race. Since their intellectual life is unquestionably grounded with its main root in rationalism, theirs might be the danger of absorption in utilitarian interests. But from such philistinism they are saved by intellectual ambition of an uncommon order. Their utilitarianism is strongly tempered with a keen spiritual inquisitiveness. Nor are they destitute of high moral aspirations. In this combination of practical sense with idealism and emotional capacity the Norwegians present perhaps one of the purest and most clear-cut types of Teutonic race character.

However, the national physiognomy of the Norwegians is also beclouded by some rather shady features, and lest Ibsen's hostile attitude to his countrymen appear absurdly prejudiced, it should be remembered that their

energies were still in abeyance when he gained his first
impressions. The national efficiency had not surged up
to its proper level till some time after *The League of Youth*
and *Brand* and *Peer Gynt* were written. The gradual steps
of the inflexible policy of progress were not perceptible
to the vision of the extremist. He saw only the detestable
"Norwegian circumspection" which made him declare
on one occasion that the object of these people was not to
be men but — Englishmen! So Ibsen, never blessed with
great patience or leniency, under the sting of experiences
from which he never quite recovered, dwelt overmuch on
the darker traits of his countrymen.

The attitudes of mind discerned by Ibsen as dominant
in the Norwegian character are those depicted and
satirized in *Brand* and *Peer Gynt*. They may be indicated
as follows: In the first place, an overdevelopment of the
critical faculties (as though this had not been Ibsen's
own besetting fault!). This predisposition to approach
every object with a withering analytical skepticism is too
likely to paralyze the will power. It leads to halfhearted-
ness in action, intolerance for the acts of others, and a
prying suspicion constantly on the rampage. No very
great safeguard lies in the supposable compensation for
this defect, the Norwegians' alleged love of truth. For
its effect is neutralized by indiscretion, extremism, and a
lacking sense of proportion; the torch of truth works
mischief in the hands of cranks and fanatics. In the
second place, Ibsen finds as an unexpected logical corol-
lary of hypercriticism and fanatical veracity, and at the
same time a saving antidote against these, the widespread
existence of national self-satisfaction; that same smug,

squat complacency, by the way, against which that other great Norwegian, Björnstjerne Björnson (1832–1910), raises his voice in *The Fishermaiden*. All traits and things Norwegian, be they never so undesirable or outright unworthy, are respected as though they were invaluable national assets. The self-infatuation is no doubt fostered by the geographical isolation of the country and the smallness of its towns,—although the phenomenon is not necessarily unknown in very large and populous countries. Finally, between the uncritical and ultra-critical, the uncompromising and complaisant attitudes, public life would seem to be thrown into a state of perpetual moral evasion. And it is this fundamental untruthfulness of the public life that serves as the background of Ibsen's earlier dramas.

Henrik Ibsen, for his part, was placed by lineage as well as evolution beyond the limitations of the strictly national Norwegian temper, be that whatever it may. His own statement regarding his expanding sense of ethnological relationship is to this effect: "I believe that national consciousness is on the point of dying out, and that it will be replaced by racial consciousness: I myself, at least, have passed through this evolution. I began by feeling myself a Norwegian; I developed into a Scandinavian, and now I have arrived at Teutonism." [1] It is a declaration that will not startle anybody who has glanced at Ibsen's pedigree. The allegation that there flowed not a drop of pure Norwegian blood in Ibsen's veins may be left for experts in eugenics to settle to their satisfaction; but that there were German, Scotch, and Danish strains

[1] *C*, p. 420.

in his make-up, there can be no doubt; and the German element would seem to have predominated, since back of the parents we find, with but few exceptions, his forbears on both sides of the family to have been Germans. The enthusiastic acceptance of Ibsen by the Germans as a German seems therefore quite intelligible, and there is no need for the cry of "Ausländerei," i.e., predilection for things alien, which is still raised by provincially minded patriots against every recognition of foreign merit. A closer examination of records, in particular a study of the autobiographical material, reveals a fact not mentioned in that letter to Brandes, namely that Ibsen's pan-Scandinavian sympathies preceded, even as they followed, the narrower patriotic state of mind into which he fell for a brief spell under the influence of his friend Björnson. We have it from Ibsen as well as from other great men, that love of country is only a transition stage in the progress of ethics. His Scandinavianism turned scornfully against Norway when she left Denmark unaided in the clutches of the German foe. He could not bear the thought of living in his country after that. Prolonged residence in Germany softened his strong anti-German feelings. Germany's heroic struggle for unity elicited his increasing admiration, and the solidification of many puny governments into a magnificent world-power made him take confidence in the historic mission of the Empire. The effect was not unlike that produced on the great Swiss novelist Konrad Ferdinand Meyer (1825–1898), who till 1870 wavered in his spiritual allegiance between the French and the Germans.

In 1872, when the first German translations of his

works appeared, — *The Pretenders*, *Brand*, and *The League of Youth* all at once, — his change of mind towards Germany as a whole was completed; but Prussia he continued to hate, for annexing Schleswig-Holstein. Even his attitude towards Germany as a whole underwent several relapses, as when in a stirring poem, *Northern Signals* ("Nordens Signaler," September, 1872),[1] he invoked the spirits of the fallen Danes against Björnson's pan-Germanic agitation. But in 1875 he wrote a poem celebrating the German union, and in 1876, in the preface to the German edition of *The Vikings*, Ibsen himself discusses "unser gesamtgermanisches Leben," — our common Germanic existence. His feeling was changed. "The universality of the Germanic nature and the Germanic mind predestines it to a future empire of the world. My having been allowed to take part in these currents I clearly and deeply feel that I owe to my having entered into the life of German society." [2] He was deeply impressed with the triumphant force of German discipline. To this large racial ideal he remained true without any slavish repression of his personal instincts and judgments. In his sympathies more than one people was embraced. In fact he could not have made so amazing an appeal to the whole world, had he not become ultimately a citizen of the whole world.

> No patriot was he. Both for Church and State
> A fruitless tree. But there, on the upland ridge,
> In the small circle where he saw his calling,
> There he was great, because he was himself.[3]

[1] *M*, vol. iii, p. 136.   [2] *SNL*, p. 114.
[3] *Peer Gynt*, vol. iv, p. 217.

It is very noteworthy how convincingly, yet without
detriment to its cosmopolitan bearing, Ibsen's work
reflects and echoes the life of his own, to us quite
unfamiliar, home-land. The *données* of his plays are
invariably Norwegian. In no single instance are his
figures homeless, phantoms from a dreamer's no-man's
land, though in their personal appearance and in their
ways they do impress us as exotic. Ibsen's art, far from
giving "to airy nothing a local habitation," worked from
the life model. Now, his models came with few exceptions
from crabbed social surroundings. It may be put down
as a limitation of his craft that in the delineation of minor
characteristics Ibsen could never get away from these
quaint provincial patterns. To their origin the "strange-
ness" of his figures is chiefly due. Their peculiarity cannot be wholly accounted for except through what Mr.
Arthur Balfour in his remarkable book *Foundations of
Belief* calls the "psychologic climate." Ibsen had a keen
sense of the importance of environment upon character,
and since to the end of his days he sensed life under a
local species, the fullest appreciation of such figures as
Mortensgaard or Dr. Relling is hardly possible to those
who do not know Norway. By the social background of
his plays we are perpetually reminded that he came from
a smallish country and that he had spent the formative
portion of his life among men of small affairs in places
where everybody knows everybody's business and respect
for public opinion amounts mainly to fear of the neighbors' tongues. In this suburban atmosphere the social
dramas of Ibsen are altogether steeped. In his book,
Zur Kritik der Moderne, Hermann Bahr cleverly draws

this distinction: Ibsen's intellect is European, but his senses are Norwegian. Hence arises the anomaly of gigantic thoughts being evolved by pygmies, and of great questions being debated by petty bourgeois to whom they must be alien.

And just as this oppressive social environment with its petty interests, its local jealousies and envies, its bickerings and backbitings, is essential to a satisfactory understanding of Ibsen's people, so again the strictly natural setting of the locality, the Norwegian landscape, is inseparable from their meaning. In lifelong exile he remained a "Heimatkünstler." His works, fashioned in foreign lands and for Germans and Englishmen as much as for Scandinavians, are in outward seeming home-made and made for home consumption. The images of home were projected by the distance only the more vividly on his memory. Among the marble splendors of the ancient world, along the sunny stretches of the Roman Campagna, his inner eye wandered back over the wide expanse of the sea or over the bleak and icy mountains of the Northern land. Thus a cold but bracing air of regional reality blows through the structures reared by a detached cosmopolitan's fancy. A few of Ibsen's scenic directions may be set down to illustrate the point. In *The Lady from the Sea*, we have: Dr. Wangel's house, with a large veranda, on the left — a view of the fjords with high mountain ranges and peaks in the distance. In *Little Eyolf*: At the back a sheer cliff, an extensive view over the fjord. In *When We Dead Awaken*: At the back a view over the fjord, right out to sea, with headlands and small islands in the distance. In *The Vikings at Helgeland*: A rocky coast running precipi-

tously down to the sea at the back . . . Far out to the
right the sea dotted with reefs and skerries on which the
surf is running high. A still better example is furnished
by the entire fourth act of *Peer Gynt*.

It is not without a biographical interest that Ibsen at
one time longed to become a painter and that he wielded
the brush rather insistently till about his thirtieth year.
Records of these crude artistic efforts exist in the form
of some rather hard and stiff landscapes composed in the
"classic-romantic" method of that day. The Norwegian
landscape also enters from the first into the obvious
higher significance of his writings. Herein consists perhaps the most precious heritage to the poet from his
country. From *Paa Vidderne* (1859–60),[1] the forerunner
of *Brand*,^c to the *Dramatic Epilogue*, the highland sym-
bolizes the heroic or sublime aspects of life, the alpine
peaks its visions splendid, as the lowland represents the
commonplace. In *Love's Comedy*, for instance, the poet
saves himself from philistinism by flight to the mountains.
The outward phenomenon of nature is with Ibsen a
symbol of inner truth. Life on the heights is ordained to
be lonesome and forbidding, yet withal free, spacious,
and salutary. It is well to remember that the scenic
motifs are never fortuitous with Ibsen, but of a fixed and
easily discernible importance. And this symbolistic
propensity, which was practiced from the start, helps the
student the better to understand the main stages in the
poet's evolution, above all his early romanticism, vague,
florid, and remote, which, having receded for a long while
in favor of a firmer, clearer, but also colder and drier

[1] *M*, vol. iii, pp. 42–54.

conception of life, was resumed later on so unmistakably with the lyric mood of his declining years. As early as 1857, in his essay on the *Kaempevise* ("Hero-Song"),[1] Ibsen had declared: "The romantic view of life concedes to rationalism its *raison d'être* and its value, but alongside of it, beyond it, and clear through it passes the mystery, the puzzle, the miracle." The return to romanticism is clearly traceable in the technical changes of Ibsen's work. In the final stage of his career he was a devotee of symbolism surpassed among contemporaries only by his own disciple, Maurice Maeterlinck.

[1] *SW*, vol. I, pp. 337–60.

CHAPTER II

EARLY LIFE AND WORKS

THE life of Henrik Ibsen offers small yield to biographical hero-worship, for in its exterior aspects it was singularly uneventful, almost dull. The briefest and barest outline will have to suffice for our purposes. He was born on March 20, 1828, — in the same year with Tolstoy, — at Skien, a small town on the southeast coast of Norway, important only as a shipping-post for timber, and otherwise the very paradigm of a solemn, somnolent, and multifariously uninteresting country town; a typical home of all the mournful virtues of Philistia, and correspondingly replete with the meannesses and pretensions that are anatomized later on by the unsparing blade of Ibsen's satire. "Stockmanns Gaard," the house where little Henrik Johan gave his first shriek of indignation, was auspiciously surrounded by certain tenebrous institutions for the improvement and protection of society: the church, the public pillory, the jail, the madhouse, the Latin High School, etc.[a] Mr. Gosse warns the tourist that over this stern prospect he can no longer sentimentalize, for the whole of this part of Skien was burned down in 1886, "to the poet's unbridled satisfaction." "The inhabitants of Skien," he said with grim humor, "were quite unworthy to possess my birthplace." [b]

Reared in the affluence of a patrician household, he suffered an evil fall from fortune at the age of eight, when his father lost nearly all of his property. From this time forth till he was well past the middle of his life he did not get out of the clutches of wretched, grinding poverty. His friend, Christopher Lorenz Due, gives the following picture of young Ibsen's destitute circumstances while at Grimstad: "He must have had an exceptionally strong constitution, for when his financial conditions compelled him to practice the most stringent economy, he tried to do without underclothing, and finally even without stockings. In these experiments he succeeded; and in winter he went without an overcoat." Embittered by his early struggle for existence, how could he escape a stern and sombre view of life? Vividly the grievous experience entered into his youthful poetry. In one of his earliest poems mankind is divided into favored guests blithely seated at the banquet of life, and miserable outsiders freezing in the street, condemned to look on through the window. Yet candid references to his childhood and adolescence, with their bitter disenchantments, are not in the manner of this taciturn poet.

His own desire to be sent to an art school abroad was not realizable, and at fifteen he was apprenticed to an apothecary at Grimstad. Here his life was still more penned up than before. But as the apothecary's shop in such towns serves as a favorite resort for the numerous male gossips and busybodies of the stamp of Mr. Daniel Heire (*The League of Youth*), it afforded the lad, over his pills and pestle, abundant opportunity for watching people in their amusing variety of tricks and manners. He practiced his satirical gift in many spiteful epigrams and lampoons on the worthy burghers. To the end of his career he loved to spy out of a safe corner on the unwary, gloating over each unconscious self-revelation conveyed by speech and gesture, and hoarding it up in the iron safe of his memory for opportune use. The oft-drawn picture rises up, by force of association, of the aged dramatist seated with an air of impenetrable reserve and in perpetual silence in his chosen nook at the "Grand Café" in Christiania, his malicious little eyes, armored with gold-rimmed spectacles and masked behind an outspread news-sheet, leveled fixedly upon the tell-tale mirror on the opposite wall. As is the case with all great realists, he had an insatiable curiosity for trifles. This was abetted by extraordinary powers of observation. "He thought it amazing," so Mr. Gosse tells us,[c] "that people could go into a room and not notice the pattern of the carpet, the color of the curtains, the objects on the walls"; these being details which he could not help observing and retaining in his memory. This trait comes out in his copious and minute stage-directions and in his well-known insistence on the details of the setting. For instance, at the first Munich performance of *A Doll's House* he criticized the wall-paper of Helmer's living-room because it interfered with the "Stimmung." But in course of artistic experience he learned to be equally observant of the recondite peculiarities of men. He had a microscopical eye for human character. The grosser seizure of superficial traits was aided in his case by a closeness and accuracy of mind-reading comparable to the clairvoyancy of the great Russian novelist Dostojevsky (1821–1881).

The pharmaceutical occupation had been chosen because it afforded Ibsen the future possibility of the

professional study of medicine. Arduous self-preparation
for the university was resorted to in place of the regular
schooling. In course of learning Latin, he was fired, by
the reading of Cicero and Sallust, to a first creative effort;
this resulted in the tragedy of *Catilina*. He went to
Christiania in 1850, but failed in the entrance examination to the University. The raw pedagogical philosophy
of the hour is free to point with grinning satisfaction to
Ibsen's failure as an argument against the value of col-
lege entrance examinations. A safer inference would be
Ibsen's unfitness for the learned professions. He clung
obstinately, to the end of his life, to an unbookishness
singular in a man of letters, and remained stubbornly
incognizant of the works even of his greatest contemporaries, such as Tolstoy and Zola. In his intellectual
interest everything else dwindled before the study of
living human beings.

In 1850 Ibsen's first play, *Kaempehöjen* ("The Warrior's Hill "), was brought before the public. He had now
drifted into the precarious existence of a literary man.
He became co-editor of an ephemeral revolutionary sheet
which never reached a round hundred of subscribers, and
this connection almost brought him behind prison bars in
the period of reaction after the turbulent year of 1848.
Some writers have wondered why to such a mere tyro at
the theatrical business, a youngster of twenty-three without experience and without any tangible and properly cer-
tified attainments, there should have come all at once a
call to leadership in a high and serious cause. Before the
starveling Bohemian all at once the gates are flung open
to a congenial career. Ole Bull calls him to the artistic

directorship of the newly founded "National Theatre" at Bergen (1851). As a matter of fact, the "National Theatre," in spite of its high-sounding name, was an extremely modest concern. The annual salary of about two hundred and fifty dollars attached to Ibsen's position indicates plainly enough the limited sphere of his dramaturgical activity. In Bergen he stayed till 1857. As a dramatic author he contributed to the national venture, besides *The Warrior's Hill*, the following works: in 1853, *St. John's Eve*; in 1856, *The Feast at Solhaug*; in 1857, a revised version of *Olaf Liljekrans*, this having been already sketched out in 1850. None of these juvenile exercises in playwriting is comparable to his first real drama, his parting gift to Bergen, *Lady Inger of Östraat* (1855).[d]

Ibsen's one lucky strike at Bergen was his marriage (1858) to Susannah Daae Thoresen, daughter of the rector and rural dean at Bergen. Mrs. Ibsen deserves a front place among the capable and long-suffering wives of men of genius.[1] Simply to have endured for full half a century the company of this exacting and exasperatingly unsocial creature bespeaks the calm endurance of a saint. But not only did she contrive to bear with the bluntnesses and edges of his character, she learned to make him happy, and stranger still, to be happy herself in the security of his captured affection.

From 1857 till 1862 Ibsen held successively at the two theatres of Christiania posts similar in responsibilities

---

[1] For a casual estimate by Ibsen of his wife cf. *C*, p. 199; also the poem *To the Only One*, of which a fine German translation by Ludwig Fulda is found in *SW*, vol. x, pp. 10–12.

and privations to that at Bergen. Certainly in this prolonged managerial connection with the theatre lies the chief explanation of his masterful stage-craft.*

In 1864 Ibsen shook the dust of Norway from his feet. The reasons will later be touched upon. After spending one month in Copenhagen, he journeyed direct to Rome. He lived there for a while, and elsewhere in Italy, then took up his residence in Germany (1868), living for the most part in Dresden and Munich, with further visits to the South, and regular annual flights to his favorite summer haunts in the Tyrol. The self-imposed exile during which he knew no permanent home and lived, practically, with his trunk always packed, lasted, with two short breaks, till 1891. Ibsen is the sole instance known to me of a writer of the first magnitude the bulk of whose literary work was produced in foreign parts.

The remainder of Ibsen's life was passed in the Norwegian capital, with the brief interruption of a journey in 1898. He died on May 23, 1906, in his seventy-ninth year. The latter portion of his life had brought him, after long and hard struggles, the gratification of every conceivable ambition: wealth, distinctions, ease, celebrity as the world's recognized chief dramatist, the allegiance of a younger generation of writers, and the well-nigh frenzied gratitude of a whole nation unanimous in calling him its first citizen. But the final years were darkly clouded. For six years the poet, now mentally infirm, had to endure the tragic fate of Oswald Alving, the curse of enforced inactivity.

Ibsen was a man of striking appearance notwithstanding his shortness of stature. On powerful shoulders rose his leonine head, with a mane of recalcitrant white locks that framed an impressively high and broad-arched brow.[f] The face with its straight, compressed lips and piercing eyes revealed the whole man. He was taciturn and reserved, except with intimates; yet on occasion frank to the point of harshness; anything but good-natured, in fact rather querulous and occasionally a bit petulant.[1]

A brief survey of Ibsen's earliest works may help us to reach the beginnings of his slow but amazing development as an artist, and as a social thinker and critic. The works here classed as juvenile are now long dead and forgotten; their attempted resuscitation during the last decade was an act of piety on the part of enthusiasts, but they could not be redeemed for the stage. Still they are unquestionably of great interest for literary history, forming as they do a species of prelude of the lifework of a great poet. The most potent influence upon the conception and style of these dramas was that of the Danish poet Adam Öhlenschläger (1779–1850), leader of the romanticist movement in Scandinavia. Next to him the Norwegian prose writer Mauritz Ch. Hansen (1794–1842), also a romanticist, should be mentioned;[g] of foreign writers Schiller was the one most familiar to Ibsen at the earliest stage of his development.

It is not quite clear that Ibsen became fully conscious in his youth of the extraordinary poetic gifts that dwelt within him. Certainly the "lyric cry" was not overpoweringly strong in him. He never excelled as a song writer. In the epic *genre* the metrical story of *Terje Vigen*

---

[1] He gave an amusing exhibition of this trait while a member of the Scandinavian Society of Rome. Cf. *SW*[II], vol. i, pp. 179–83.

(1860) [1] was his only noteworthy effort. His many pro-
logues and other poems of occasion demonstrate, in the
main, nothing more than an exceptional facility in the
handling of verse and rime.[h]

In the narrative field he was practically unproductive.
Of the projected novel *The Prisoner at Agershuus,* a mere
shred of a beginning reached fruition.[2] For Ibsen, poetical
material turned spontaneously into drama, as he himself
informs us. "The inorganic comes first, then the organic.
First dead nature, then living. The same obtains in art.
When a subject first rises up in my mind I always want
to make a story of it, — but it manages to grow into a
drama." [3]

It is with Ibsen's plays that we are most concerned.
As regards the early works of that kind, there is a certain
negative quality, quite astonishing in the light of later
development, which they have in common. They cling
to accepted patterns. Ibsen's technical originality was
relatively slow to develop. Without a knowledge of the
earlier specimens of his art we might well speculate on
the reason why such æsthetic Jacobinism as his could have
been endured for a dozen years by the decorous bourgeois
of Bergen and Christiania. But the fact is, Ibsen was by
no means widely out of line with the use and wont of the
theatre at this time, and so he created for himself no
difficulties in his position by balking the public sentiment.
He had not yet stepped from the leading strings of the
then acknowledged masters of the drama. A survey of
the repertory of the Norwegian Theatre of Christiania

---

[1] *M*, vol. III (*Digte*), pp. 61-71; *SW*, vol. I, pp. 69-82.
[2] *SW*[II], vol. I, pp. 149-54.   [3] *Ibid.*, p. 198.

under Ibsen's management is given in his annual Director's Report, for 1860–61. We gain an idea of the make-up of this repertory from the titles of the plays that were newly mounted during the period covered by the report: *The Wood Nymph's Home*, drama with song and dance; *Sword and Pigtail* ("Zopf und Schwert") by Gutzkow; *He drinks*, vaudeville; *A Dangerous Letter*, comedy; *A Speech*, vaudeville; *Pernille's Brief Singleness*, comedy; *The Folk of Gudbrandsdal*, drama, etc.[1]

Ibsen's first drama, *Catilina*, was never deemed worthy of actual performance. It was begun in the year of the great European uprising, 1848, finished in 1849, and published in 1850,[2] at the expense of a loyal friend and under the pen-name of "Brynjolf Bjarme"; the edition was eventually wasted, after a sale of some twenty copies more or less. The introduction to the second, greatly altered, edition (1875) reinforces the value of the work as a human document. Historical subjects were *de rigeur*, especially for budding dramatic geniuses. Ibsen's play is written for the most part in the conventional blank verse; the final portion is in rimes, each line running to from thirteen to fifteen syllables. The one thing at all remarkable in this crude treatment of a time-honored theme is the independent conception of the principal character. Ibsen wrote uninfluenced by and probably ignorant of his predecessors in the premises, from Ben Jonson to Alexandre Dumas *fils*, nor was he hampered by any attempt at unconditional adhesion to the "historical truth" of the story.

---

[1] *SW*[II], vol. I, pp. 175–79; cf. also *SW*, vol. I, p. 290 *f*.

[2] The first version of *Catilina* is found in *SW*[II], vol. I, pp. 231–316; the second version (1875) in *SW*, vol. I, pp. 537–628.

Those who agree with the assertion that Ibsen, throughout his diversified literary career, was above all things a "poet of ideas," that is, had for his chief purpose the ventilation of moral views and theories, will find valuable confirmation of the belief in the introduction to the play. It is in essence an avowal of an excess of intellectual intention. The young dramatist thinks it fair to apologize for having tampered with the characters, and pleads in extenuation his desire of giving unrestrained play to the central animating idea. He explains that his Catiline was not meant for a *hero* in the popular sense, but for a *personality*, and therefore had to be presented as an incarnate mixture of noble and base qualities. In fact, Ibsen's Catiline is widely removed from the sly, ambitious desperado of Cicero's rolling periods. Much nearer does he approach the Sallustian view of his character, — an anarchist, but from no ignoble impulse and not without a high patriotic aim. Mr. Haldane Macfall eloquently sums up his case: "An heroic Catiline, a majestic and vigorous soul, burning with enthusiasm for the great heroic past, horrified at the rottenness of his age, raising a revolt at the corrupt state, but too steeped in that rottenness himself to be able to save the age." Singlehanded he resolves to clean out the Augean stable of society; but his power for good is perverted by the instability of his nature. His lack of equilibrium between will and capacity brings this figure into conspicuous kinship with many a wrecked Titan of earlier literature; yet closer still is his spiritual affinity with the half-baked overmen of innumerable recent German works, as Hauptmann's Meister Heinrich, to instance only one.

It is certainly noteworthy how early in his career Ibsen was fascinated by the virtue of self-reliance militantly advancing against the authority of state, church, and family. But at this stage he could not draw such characters from life as when he came to compose *An Enemy of the People* or *John Gabriel Borkman*. The female characters by their complete unrealness betray the novice hand, though they herald Ibsen's notorious division of his women into two distinct classes, namely, women controlled by their heart, and women controlled by their will. And here, too, at the very outset of Ibsen's dramatical career, we find his hero in the characteristic dilemma between two women of the different types. The same antithesis as here between the angelic Aurelia and the demonic Furia occurs with regularity in nearly all the later plays, as in *Lady Inger*, where Inger Gyldenlöve and her daughter Eline, in *The Vikings*, where Hjördis and Dagny, in *The Feast at Solhaug*, where Margit and Signe are placed in sharp juxtaposition.

The youthful plays are strongly under historical influence, but from Roman history the interest soon switches off to themes of a national Scandinavian provenience. The first which actually gained a momentary foothold on the stage was the one-act play entitled *The Hero's Mound* ("Kaempehöjen," 1851). It was the *rifacimento* of *The Norsemen* ("Normannerne"), written in 1849. Ibsen justly held this play in low opinion and would not consent to its being included in the complete edition of his works.[1]

---

[1] After Ibsen's death, however, it was made accessible through the publication of the *Efterladte Skrifter*, by Koht and Elias; cf. also *SW*, vol. ii, pp. 1-33.

Yet it shows a certain fitness for the theatre sadly
absent in *Catilina*. The manuscript of this short dramatic sketch having been irrecoverably lost, likewise the
serial reprint of it in a newspaper of 1854, the prompting copy preserved in the library of the theatre at Bergen
has had to serve Ibsen's latest editors in lieu of a more
authentic original. The playlet was written in blank
verse, with several lyrics interspersed. Originally the
scene was laid in Normandy, but later it was moved to
Sicily. The time is shortly before the Christianization of
the Norwegians. And the fundamental idea was to show
how the civilization of the period moved up from the
South to the North. The heroine, Blanka, in the restrain-
ing influence exercised by her goodness and virtue on the
barbarians, seems reminiscent of Goethe's Iphigenia.
The tone is decidedly romantic, and both in the conception and the phrasing there is to be observed along with a
pronounced lack of individual style an almost slavish
imitation of the manner of Adam Öhlenschläger. Obviously Ibsen was now kindled with enthusiasm for the
past of his native land. This is not the only time that an
expedition of Vikings forms the theme of a drama by
Ibsen. In order to understand the range of his images
and ideas it should be borne in mind that modern Dano-
Norwegian poetry derives its themes mainly from three
sources, so far as it does not deal explicitly with contemporary or with historical subjects. The sources are
the Eddas and Sagas, the ancient folk-songs, and finally
the works of the great Danish dramatist Ludwig Holberg
(1684–1754). To the Bergen period belongs furthermore
The Night of St. John ("Sankthansnatten"), a fairy

play in three acts dating from 1852 (played 1853).[1] In craftsmanship it shows no material advance. On the stage it proved a flat failure, and but for the rescuing hands of the editors of the posthumous works it would have remained in the oblivion to which its author had consigned it. The story bears a popular character and is full of good ideas, but is clumsily executed. An outline of the plot will serve a use by pointing to the contrast between Ibsen's crude beginnings and his subsequent mastery. The content, it will be observed, is national, but the technique is palpably French, in accordance with the contemporary fashion in drama. Ibsen's chief guiding star at Bergen and Christiania seems to have been Scribe, as appears especially from the technical construction of *Love's Comedy*. But his own independent manner is already discernible in certain features of *The Night of St. John*, notably in that favorite contrivance of his, the unveiling of a past family secret for the denouement of the plot, used so effectively in *Lady Inger*, *A Doll's House*, *Ghosts*, *Rosmersholm*, etc. In later plays several of the dramatic concepts of *The Night of St. John* are repeated to better advantage. The resemblance of its fantastic romanticism to *Peer Gynt* is self-evident. The play introduces Mrs. Berg, her daughter Juliane, a son, and a stepdaughter Anne, a sweet poetic soul thought to be unbalanced because of her fantastic imagination and belief in elfs and trolls. Juliane is affianced to the impecunious student Johannes Birk, who falls in love with Anne. Young Berg brings his friend Paulsen home with him. The latter and Juliane fall promptly in love. On

[1] *SW*[II], vol. I, pp. 355–428.

the festal night of St. John the young people stroll to a
woody hill in order to enjoy the bonfires. A magic potion
mixed with the holiday punch makes the region seem
enchanted. The hillside bursts open and discloses to their
view the Mountain King with his gnomes and sprites. But
this and the ensuing witchery is experienced only by two
of the young people, Johannes and Anne, thanks to their
capacity for deeper feelings.*j* The young "poet" Paulsen
and the sentimental doll Juliane see none of it. The ill-
assorted couple Juliane and Johannes dissolve their en-
gagement. In the final winding-up Birk marries Anne
and Juliane takes the æsthetic *poseur* Paulsen, a forerunner of Stensgaard in *The League of Youth*. The meagre
little play, with its naïve fable which belongs in a class
with the *White Grouse of Justedal*,[1] harks back to an earlier inspiration perhaps than any other of Ibsen's works.
For in the reminiscences of his school days, while speaking of the gay social doings of the little town, Ibsen dwells
particularly on the joyous celebration of St. John's Night,
when the general merriment was apt to grow boisterous,
and good-natured pranks would be indulged in with a fair
degree of impunity.

[1] *SW*[II], vol. i, pp. 319–54.

CHAPTER III

HISTORY AND ROMANCE

THE first hint of extraordinary dramatic force is contained in his next play, *Lady Inger of Östraat* ("Fru Inger til Östraat," 1855). Work on this historical tragedy started at Bergen, in 1854; on January 2 of the following year it was performed there for the first time. A few copies were printed in 1857, and a somewhat revised edition, with an interesting preface, came out in 1874. The influence of German romanticism is quickly discovered in this tragedy; quite in line with it is the lavish use of balladistic notions and phrases. More than enough has perhaps been said about the mechanical adjustment of this play to the demands of the regnant school of the drama. But *Lady Inger* is just Ibsen's first "well-made" piece, not by any means his last or only one. Not till the beginning of his middle period does he free himself from that governing influence whose hold upon him is unquestioned up to the last act of *A Doll's House*. In all these plays, then, not merely in *Lady Inger*, must we expect to find and do in fact find superabundance of external incident, plots teeming with complications and surprises, and a pertinacious use of "telling" entrances and effective curtains. In *Lady Inger* the intricacies are so great as to interfere with the intelligibility of the dramatic process; the mind of the spectator is hopelessly confused by the continual *quid pro quos* and cross-purposes which a mere reader of the play may reason out at his leisure. And surely it is our curiosity and excitement that wax from scene to scene rather than our human sympathy, as should be the case in true drama. Even the vice of ranting might be charged here against a poet who in his later course abstained severely from rhetorical invective. To make full the measure of his sins against art, Ibsen manipulated the plot in a decidedly sensational manner. The intrigue is far-fetched, the catastrophe — a mother causing her own son to be slain, through ignorance of his identity — harrowing rather than tragical, because it lacks a sound psychological foundation.

Yet with all these manifest imperfections we can date from *Lady Inger of Östraat* a prophetic advance in one domain of dramaturgy, namely, in the art of character painting. *Lady Inger* is unquestionably Ibsen's first great tragedy of character, properly speaking. Two masterly figures, created by the poet's imagination, are shown in play and counterplay, each bent upon overmatching the other: Inger, the mother torn betwixt love for her child and her land, a woman of masculine temper and giant force of will; and Nils Lykke, the Danish knight, wily master of politics, ruthless and irresistible vanquisher of women. It is diamond cut diamond. Ibsen wove only the background of this drama from historical material, his object being to throw into strong relief a private, not a political, tragedy. He did his utmost, so he tells us,[1] to familiarize himself with the manners and customs, with the thoughts and feelings, and also the language of the men of those days. Against the hopeless national decay

---

[1] Vol. I, p. 189; *SW*, vol. II, pp. 152-53.

at the beginning of the sixteenth century he makes his heroine stand forth, "the greatest personage of her day," in tragical moral grandeur far surpassing the historic Fru Inger Gyldenlöve. The author's sentiment is frankly nationalistic, his argument pointed against Denmark. A woman can frighten that rotten state, and is only prevented from her patriotic purpose by the plight of her child in the hands of the enemy. The personal characters and fates make no pretense of being authentic. Personalities are freely transformed or invented, as for instance, Eline Gyldenlöve, a fascinating girl, proud and self-possessed, yet capable of passionate self-abandonment. In their psychological foundations they are rightfully modernized, for what, indeed, could be a Hecuba to us in her stark historic impersonality? Thus *Lady Inger* harbors a presage of the coming social tragedies, made more emphatic by the fact that this play, contrary to the traditions and conventions, was composed in prose.

Despite this foreshowing of a realistic tendency, Ibsen's genius continues to travel in the romantic direction. His next play was called *The Feast at Solhaug* ("Gildet paa Solhaug," 1856). It was written in the summer of 1855 and saw the footlights in 1856 on the second day of January, like all of Ibsen's Bergen plays, since on that day the founding of the theatre was commemorated.[a] About the same time it was published and accorded a very warm reception both by the audiences and readers. It is far less gloomy than *Lady Inger*. It is even, on the whole, written in a genial mood, as cheerful as it ever lay in Ibsen's power to be. A comedy, however, it is not, — rather an attempt at a "Schauspiel" of a quasi-lyrical order. Either

for this reason or perhaps because he found it more difficult at this time to handle prose than verse in drama of
the lighter *genre,* Ibsen returned to verse, but aside from
a fairly normal recurrence of four beats to the line the
metre is extremely varied and irregular. In artistic merit
the new play dropped behind *Lady Inger.* In fact, *The
Feast at Solhaug* was one of a few achievements of his
"Lehrjahre" which Ibsen explicitly disowned, for a
while at least, and which he never acknowledged to be
in any degree representative of his ability.

From the author's preface to the second edition (1883)
may be gathered valuable information in regard to the
genesis of this play and its import for the trend of Ibsen's
artistic progress. His statement is here given with some
abridgments.

In 1854 I had written *Lady Inger of Östraat.* This was a task
which had obliged me to devote much attention to the literature
and history of Norway during the Middle Ages. . . . The period,
however, does not present much material suitable for dramatic
treatment. Consequently I soon deserted it for the saga period.
But the sagas of the kings did not attract me greatly; at that
time I was unable to put the quarrels between kings and chief-
tains, parties and clans, to any dramatic purpose. This was to
happen later. In the Icelandic "family" sagas, on the other
hand, I found in abundance the human material required for the
moods, conceptions, and thoughts which at that time occupied
me, or were, at least, more or less distinctly present in my mind.
. . . In the pages of these family chronicles, with their variety
of scenes and of relations between man and man, between woman and woman, in short, between human beings, I met a personal, eventful, really vital existence; and as the result of my in-
tercourse with all these distinctly individual men and women,
there presented themselves to my mind's eye the first rough,

indistinct outlines of *The Vikings at Helgeland*. Various obstacles intervened. . . . My mood of the moment was more in
harmony with the literary romanticism of the Middle Ages than
with the deeds of the sagas, with poetical than with prose composition, with the word-melody of the ballad than with the characterization of the saga. Thus it happened that the fermenting,
formless design for the tragedy, *The Vikings at Helgeland*, transformed itself temporarily into the lyric drama, *The Feast at Solhaug*.[1]

The shifting of his interest from the sagas to the ballads
was quickened by the impression received from the study
of M. B. Landstad's collection of Norwegian folksongs.[b]
Ibsen points out in the concluding paragraph of the preface, how under those circumstances the female principals
of the Viking tragedy, that was already maturing in his
mind, spontaneously transformed themselves into the
sisters Margit and Signe of the other nascent drama; how
Sigurd, the seafaring hero, changed into the knightly
minstrel Gudmund Alfson, whose relation to the two sisters is much the same as that of Sigurd to Hjördis and
Dagny. The writer ends with the following emphatic
declaration: —

The play under consideration, *The Feast at Solhaug*, like all
my other dramatic works, is an inevitable outcome of the tenor
of my life at a certain period. It had its origin within and was
not the result of any outward impression or influence.

The resemblance of the plot to *The Vikings* springs into
prominence upon a closer comparison than would here be
in place. The dramatic conflict is brought on by the visit
of Gudmund, after long absence, to the house of Bengt, to
whom Margit is bound in unhappy marriage. Her love

[1] Vol. i, pp. 183-92.

for the playmate of her youth is violently awakened, but his love now turns toward the younger sister. Margit's attempt against her husband is stayed by the hand of a gracious fate, which also sets her free by making her a widow. Signe and Gudmund join hands while Margit retires to a nunnery.

In order of his works the satirical comedy *Norma, or The Love of a Politician* ("Norma, eller En Politikers Kjaerlighed ")[1] followed next. It is called a musical tragedy in three acts, but is in fact nothing more than a brief political skit in the guise of a libretto.

Olaf Liljekrans (1857) had been roughly sketched in 1850, under a different title, before Ibsen had completed his twenty-second year, but was not finished until six years afterward. It, too, was written in verse, imitating the measures of the ancient heroic ballads for whose rugged stride and swing Ibsen at this time cherished a great liking. It is, however, one of Ibsen's least successful dramas.[c] The strong national-historic bent of the piece, whose ultimate version was called for the hero of one of the most famous of the Kaempeviser, was already indicated in the designation of "national drama" which Ibsen bestowed on the earlier version. This torso, lately published by the literary executors of the poet, bears the title *The White Grouse of Justedal* ("Justedalsrypa").[2] It consists of about one act and a half, all that was written of the four acts intended. The dialogue is mixed of verse and

---

[1] *Efterladte Skrifter*, vol. I, pp. 76–86; *SW*II, vol. I, pp. 21–31.

[2] *Rypen i Justedal, Efterl. Skr.*, vol. I, pp. 339 *ff.* In German: *Das Schneehuhn in Justedalen*. National-Schauspiel in vier Akten von Brynjolf Bjarme. 1850. *SW*II, vol. I, pp. 319–53. (The same pen-name was used in *Catilina*.)

prose. But the theme was realized once more under the abridged title *The Wild Bird* ("Fjeldfuglen," 1859), "a romantic opera in three acts by Henrik Ibsen."[1] Only a brief fragment of this libretto is preserved. The action of *The White Grouse*, as well as of *Olaf Liljekrans*, is out and out romantic in its conception. The hackneyed theme of the hostile brothers is utilized for the previous history of the characters. A masterful personality is introduced in the old yeoman Bengt, who is pursued by a guilt-laden conscience because he has evilly contrived the disinheritance of his elder brother. The latter, with his wife, has gone into exile and passed out of the story. Bengt's son, Björn, by his father's wish is to marry Merete for her property, but she is in love with young farmer Einar. Björn for his part meets and loves a wonderful maiden named Alfhild, an orphan dwelling in solitude amidst the beauties of nature, on terms of wondrous familiarity with the flowers and creatures of the woods. But one human being has she seen since her parents died: an aged minstrel of wonderful skill. Woe to the house that does not bid him welcome. Alfhild, of course, is the daughter of the lost Alf. The winding-up of the story is easily divined.

The Vikings in Helgeland ("Haermaendene paa Helgeland," 1858) was published after being rejected by leading Scandinavian theatres. Under Ibsen's management it was given at Christiania, November 24, 1858. The leading theatres in the Scandinavian countries first opened to this play in 1875, and only after Ibsen's social problem

---

[1] *SW*II, vol. II, pp. 3–24. It was to be set to music by Udbye. In the list of *dramatis personæ* occurs Thorgejr, a minstrel who reappears in *The Pretenders.*

plays had compelled international attention was this heroic drama given an occasional trial abroad. In Berlin it was staged in 1890. Before that, the great Viennese tragédienne, Charlotte Wolter, had triumphantly impersonated the part of Hjördis by virtue of her conquering vehemence of temper, whereas Ellen Terry appears to have scored barely a *succès d'estime* for her more moderated performance of the part.

Critical opinion of the play runs the wide gamut from "sorry failure" to "superb achievement." Whether or no the latter estimate is extravagant, Mr. Archer's statement that *The Vikings* forms a cornerstone of modern Norwegian literature, along with Björnson's peasant idyll *Synnöve Solbakken*, is not to be gainsaid. Ibsen began his tragedy under the then reigning Helleno-romantic influence; of course he started out in verse, in writing which he had by this time acquired an extraordinary facility. Fortunately he discerned very soon a far fitter vehicle for his poetical intentions in colloquial prose of old-time simplicity and quaintness, which aided the imagination in reconstructing the temporal environment of the plot. His diction then readily took on the ancient flavor of the Icelandic family sagas that had suggested the theme.[a] The adoption of prose was by no means a meretricious device for smoother sailing and quicker arrival, as some foolish people have been misled into thinking. And here he takes the decisive turn to a new mode of dramatic expression, that realistic terseness of an unadorned, almost naked prose dialogue, which he eventually domiciled on the stage. *The Vikings* is a singular adaptation of the Sigfrid saga. Its substance derives from the Volsung saga, but, so Ibsen

emphatically declares, only in part. He says, most signifi-
cantly, "More essentially my poem may be said to be
founded upon the various Icelandic family sagas (recorded
in the thirteenth century), in which it often seems that
the titanic conditions and occurrences of the *Nibelungenlied* and the Volsung saga have simply been reduced to
human dimensions."[1] To the form he had given much
study, as is evidenced by his essay on the heroic ballad,
mentioned before. He shared at this time, and much later
too, the prevalent view about the indispensability of the
lyric element in drama: "If the poet is to extract a dramatic work from this epic material [meaning the sagas],
he must necessarily bring into it a foreign, a lyrical element; for the drama is well known to be a higher blending
of the lyric and the epic."[2] He swerved from the sagas
to the ballad because in the latter the lyric material is
present, whereas it has to be artificially imported in the
former.

From the countless modern versions of the story of Sigfrid or Sigurd and the Nibelungs, *The Vikings in Helgeland* differs essentially in the treatment. The dramatic
possibilities of the old epic were too obvious not to have
been exploited often before. In Germany, Friedrich Hebbel did most justice to the theme, some time after Ibsen.
It was he who defined his task in dramatizing the *Nibelungenlied* as consisting simply in stripping the ancient
epic of its nondramatic, i.e., specifically epic and lyric[e] ac-
cessories. Hebbel, too, perceived with a true dramatist's
insight that the mythological apparatus of the saga, no
matter how great may be its intrinsic worth and value, is

[1] Vol. II, pp. xi–xii.   [2] *Ibid.*, pp. ix–x.

irrelevant to the tragic force of the purely human story; that consequently all the fabulous paraphernalia, dwarfs and dragons, magic hoods and rings and cinctures, can be spared without detriment to the dramatic effect. Nevertheless he was unwilling to abandon the fabulous elements for fear of losing touch with the fixed popular predilection for the theme; so the marvelous strains are saved, not in the ground melody, however, but in the accompaniment.

Ibsen went much further. Like Hebbel, he descried in the ancient tale a most attractive subject for a drama; but he gave short shrift to all its extra-natural features, and reduced the tragedy to purely human terms. By the blending of material and additions of his own the story was altered almost beyond recognition. The result is virtually a new story, but with a striking inner resemblance to the old, due to a close analogy of *motifs*. Ibsen's experiment was an extremely daring one: he did not really dramatize either the *Nibelungenlied* or the Scandinavian legends about Sigurd the Volsung. His play bodies forth the fates and actions of mere men and women, not of demons and demigods. It expresses generally an emotional life much like our own, only a degree ruder, more elemental, in consonance with the character of early Teutonic existence. The primitive flavor is religiously preserved. In its particulars the story had to be materially altered by piecing together matters originally disconnected, to account for everything by natural means. To illustrate the transformation: the legendary Sigurd breaks, by miraculous feats of valor, the ban put upon the Valkyrie Brynhild, and by means of magic deception wins her for King Gunther.

In Ibsen's play Sigurd conquers Hjördis after slaying her
sentinel, a bear of formidable strength, a deed represented as extremely difficult, to be sure, yet entirely within
the possibilities of exceptional valiancy; the ensuing deception of Hjördis is rendered feasible by the darkness of
the night. All the wonders of the saga were excised, root
and branch, with one sole exception, — when Hjördis
hears the "Aasgardsreien," i.e., the ride of the battle-
felled warriors to Valhal, and makes ready to join it, —
and even for this a natural explanation could be invented
at a pinch. Then, too, the social level of the play's persons
is considerably lowered. Gunnar, unscrupulously divested
of his royal dignity, appears in the character of a rich yeoman. One almost wonders why he, as well as Sigurd, has
been allowed to retain his name, whereas the female principals, Brynhild and Kriemhild (Guthrun), have been re-
named Hjördis and Dagny. Ibsen may have held to
those names in order to indicate the provenience of the
theme.

Having resolutely deviated from the ancient story, the
poet was free to go his own ways in the delineation of
character. Yet, here, instead of fully availing himself of
his freedom, he follows, in the main, the trail of tradition.
Thus, in view of their rather fixed psychology, the actions
of the persons do not always fit their changed conditions
and circumstances. The entire tragic crisis and catastrophe arise out of Sigurd's guilty act — the lie conspired
between him and Gunnar. But in this rendering Sigurd's
intercession for his friend is both unintelligible and unin-
telligent, through the absence of any good reason, such as
exists in the ancient versions, why Sigurd should not win

the loved woman for himself. The significant thing, however, is that at the root of the human tragedy we are shown by the poet here, for the first time, the lie as the destroyer of happiness.

Throughout the action all the figures have a stationary aspect. They are not so much individuals as types, like roughly carved figures in a game of chess, each assessed with an immutable value. Hardly a trace is here revealed of the poet's amazing art of individualization. Nevertheless he was going forward in the right path, in quest of a new style for the drama. Perhaps the diction is as crude and clumsy as is the drawing of the characters. Yet it struggles visibly, and not unsuccessfully, away from the sonorous and grandiloquent declamation in general use for the higher drama of the time. Ibsen had doubtless chastened his diction through his favorite reading, the Scripture and the sagas. Yet *The Vikings* marks only his first perceptible advance in the new direction; he did not definitely cast off the older rhetorical manner till after *Pillars of Society*. The principal advance in *The Vikings* is along constructive lines. In this respect the play leaves very little to be desired. The composition, indeed, is masterly. In a perfectly logical manner each act rears itself to a climax so spontaneous that, notwithstanding our foreknowledge of the occurrences, the interest is held in breathless suspense from start to finish. Also a certain proficiency in that laconic brevity in which Ibsen later on excelled is here noticeable for the first time. It is attained by an extremely dexterous proportioning between articulate and smothered expression; that is, by winnowing out all unessential details without omitting anything that

actually contributes to the comprehension of the source
and course of the tragedy.

In the management of the dramatic mechanism a still
greater progress is to be noted in the play with which Ibsen next began to occupy himself and in which the archa-
istic style was again used. It is this play, *The Pretenders*,
that launched Ibsen safely on the career of a world-poet,
while yet his own compatriots were blinded by their dense
suburbanism to the justice of his claims at home. As its
completion, however, was preceded by that of *Love's Comedy* ("Kaerlighedens Komedie," 1862), a chronologically
ordered review has to record a temporary artistic retrogression. This opinion is offered, however, in full recognition of the symptomatical portent of the *Comedy*. For it
is unquestionably the first of Ibsen's dramatic treatises on
social philosophy. "*Love's Comedy*," says Ibsen, "is the
forerunner of *Brand;* for in it I have represented the contrast in our state of society between the actual and the
ideal in all that relates to love and marriage."[1] The comparison with *Brand*, not at once discernible, is quite appo-
site. For in this comedy Ibsen draws for the first time the
extreme consequences of moral and intellectual consistency in its combat with the universal social sham. For
the first time, too, he gives free rein to his characteristically bellicose disposition. An earlier attempt of the theme
was made in 1860 under the title *Svanhild*.[2] The idea of
the play, undoubtedly inspired by Schopenhauer's belief that love is a delusion and his cynical assertion that
nature throws it as a mere sop to mankind in order to
secure her object, procreation, might be expressed in the

[1] *C*, pp. 123 and 237.   [2] *SW*II, vol. II, pp. 25-43.

form of a cynical syllogism: Marriage, a social necessity,
is sure death to love. Nothing is more grievous than dis-
illusionment in love. Ergo, only a conventional marriage
can be happy. And the double-barreled moral is this: If
you are in love, do not marry; if you want to marry, be
sure you are not moved by love. Consequently, if a poet
would trace love's true course, he might do worse than go
by the directions of his colleague, Falk, in *Love's Comedy*.

> You're aware,
> No curtain falls but on a plighted pair.
> Thus with the Trilogy's First Part we've reckoned;
> The Comedy of Troth-plight, Part the Second,
> Thro' five insipid Acts he has to spin,
> And of that staple, finally, compose
> Part Third, — or Wedlock's Tragedy, in prose.[1]

The satire turns a direct shaft of white light on the ful-
crum of the social apparatus. Ibsen finds that the trouble
with marriage is fundamental levity, and has the courage
to proclaim his discovery. The comedy, then, is at bot-
tom very serious. Hence the outburst of indignation with
which it was received. "The sting," says Professor C. H.
Herford in introducing his translation, "lay in the unflat-
tering veracity of the piece as a whole; in the merciless
portrayal of the trivialities of persons, or classes, high in
their own esteem; in the unexampled effrontery of bring-
ing a clergyman upon the stage."[2]

The unflagging idealist, Falk, in this play speaks
frankly for the poet fired with a holy purpose.

> Right in the midst of men the Church is founded,
> Where Truth's appealing clarion must be sounded.
> We are not called, like demigods, to gaze on
> The battle from the far-off mountain crest,

[1] Vol. I, p. 328.   [2] *Ibid.*, p. xxxix.

> But in our hearts to bear our fiery blazon,
> An Olaf's cross upon a mailéd breast,
> To look afar across the fields of flight,
> Tho' pent within the mazes of its might,
> Beyond the mirk descry one glimmer still
> Of glory — that's the call we must fulfill.[1]

To the fulfillment of this call to a noble mission marriage as a rule is antagonistic. A case in point is the divinity-student Lind, erstwhile dedicating his future to mission-ary labors in foreign parts, yet ready, so soon as he is betrothed, to nullify in a moment the higher ambition and to become a poky pedagogue at home, for the sake of bread and butter for two mouths and more.

To fulfill the "call," the superior individual must per-force "break from men, stand free, alone"; it is aston-ishing how clearly the fugue of Ibsen's social ideas is fore-sounded in the comedy.

> My four-wall-chamber poetry is done;
> My verse shall live in forest and in field,
> I'll fight under the splendor of the sun,
> *I or the Lie*— one of us two must yield.[2]

The greatest help to the man of heroic moral calibre comes ever from the obstinate courage of a woman like Svanhild: —

> If you make war on lies, I stand
> A trusty armor-bearer by your side.[3]

Of course, a danger lurks in chivalry — witness Don Quixote, — one may become a monomaniac on almost any subject; truth may become an obsession instead of a cause. The intractable Falk goes his own inexorable way, but

[1] Vol. i, p. 404.   [2] *Ibid.*, p. 405.   [3] *Ibid.*, p. 404.

with whom are we to sympathize when he meets Parson
Strawman's objection: —

> Even though you crush another's happiness?

with smiling nonchalance: —

> I plant the flower of knowledge in its place.[1]

Involuntarily the thought wanders to Gregers Werle, the
meddlesome peddler of truth, in *The Wild Duck*. Was
Plato so very wrong in wanting to banish the poet from
his republic?

Falk and Svanhild are two ideal natures attracted by a
profounder, more unworldly love than is known to the
Strawmans and Linds and Stivers, and drawn apart
again by fear of their love being cheapened in the mart of
experience. If Love is to conserve its uplifting power, it
must first have paled into a memory. The seemingly para-
doxical moral of *Love's Comedy* is that if you want to keep
love alive it behooves you to sacrifice it at its culminating
point.

> *Falk.*   But — to sever thus!
> Now, when the portals of the world stand wide, —
> When the blue spring is bending over us,
> On the same day that plighted thee my bride!
>   *Svanhild.*   Just therefore must we part. Our joys' torch-fire
> Will from this moment wane till it expire!
> And when at last our worldly days are spent,
> And face to face with our great Judge we stand,
> And, as a righteous God, he shall demand
> Of us the earthly treasure that he lent —
> Then, Falk, we cry, past power of Grace to save —
> "O Lord, we lost it going to the grave!"
>   *Falk* (*with strong resolve*).   Pluck off the ring!
>   *Svanhild* (*with fire*).   Wilt thou?

[1] Vol. I, p. 418.

> *Falk.* Now I divine!
> Thus and no otherwise canst thou be mine!
> As the grave opens into Life's Dawn-fire,
> So Love with Life may not espoused be
> Till, loosed from longing and from wild desire,
> It soars into the heaven of memory!
>   *Svanhild.* Now for this earthly life I have foregone thee, —
> But for the life eternal I have won thee! [1]

To what extent the wrathful condemnation of *Love's Comedy* was merited it would be idle to discuss. So much is certain, that it was not prompted by artistic idiosyncrasies, but was almost wholly due to bitter personal resentment. An author must not expect to fall foul of people's fixed notions and pet prejudices with impunity; least of all when not even a visible minority is ripe for enlightened views. So Ibsen had brought a hornet's nest about his ears. The Norwegian public was shocked beyond measure. Instanter whole handfuls of fingers of scorn were pointed at Ibsen's domestic affairs, — the play had been begun in the early period of his marriage, — which were misrepresented in such a light that if true they would have made any man turn pessimist. Are not even the *illuminati* apt to blur the nice distinction between a poet's personal and his vicarious experience?

> A much-discerning Public hold
> The singer generally sings
> Of personal and private things,
> And prints and sells his past for gold!

The difference between "erleben" and "durchleben," in which for Ibsen consisted the very criterion of his poetic activity,[2] was utterly missed. Wholly impercipient of

[1] Vol. I, p. 451. All the above translations are by C. H. Herford.
[2] *C*, p. 190; but in the translation the point is not well brought out.

the new literary values that ran in the trenchant lines of
the comedy, the critics saw in it only a libelous infraction
of the unquestioned all-rightness of the use and wont.
Scandal, distress, and ostracism were the immediate and
inevitable fruitage of the poet's labor. His social excom-
munication was unavoidable, — exile or expatriation a
mere question of time. In one of Mirza-Schaffy's sage
epigrams we are told that he who thinks the truth must
have his horse by the bridle, and he who speaks it must
have wings instead of arms.⁹ Falk's predicament was sym-
bolical for Ibsen's: —

> Like Israel at the Passover I stand,
> Loins girded for the desert, staff in hand.[1]

A more conciliatory author would have quitted the social drama for good as a field in which his every appearance was bound to stir up strife and bitterness. True, the
man of genius hopes and feels that the world, of whose ruling opinion and taste he is always in advance, will eventually catch up with his position; but a man like Ibsen
suspects that he will not be long marking time on the
higher standpoint gained. He will ever keep a decade in
advance of the rest, hence he and his public will never
dwell at peace in the same resting-place.[2] His first social
play had served Ibsen ill with his countrymen, and before
the discouragements on every side he had to halt. Having
shot his first bolt, he had to wait some time before he re-
newed his attack, with far greater force than before, upon
the castle of conservatism; before he again attempted a
drastic seizure of reality in its everyday aspect. His next
move would seem to indicate a return, be it permanent

[1] Vol. i, p. 409.   [2] C, p. 370.

or passing, to the earlier range of subjects for dramaturgy.

The subject-matter, then, gave him trouble in plenty. Meanwhile it is almost pathetic to observe his heroic efforts to perfect his work in respect to its form. After *The Vikings* he could not fail to realize that prose was, to say the least, a perfectly feasible and legitimate vehicle of dramatic dialogue. The subject of *Love's Comedy* even seemed downright to call for treatment in prose. Yet though his loyalty to romantic views was wearing off, it was to cost him many pangs to break for good with rime and measure. The experiment with *The Vikings* had succeeded: the archaic flavor of the colloquy saved the poetic quality. But now it was a question of couching in plain, ordinary language wit and gayety, suffused with sentiment, in a dramatized event of yesterday or to-day. Ibsen tried, and failed in the attempt. His powers were unequal to the task which required for its solution long and persistent experimentation; reluctantly he reverted to his past method and set about versifying the dialogue. Metrical speech came to him at all times with extraordinary ease and fluency.

The Pretenders ("Kongs-Emnerne," 1864) was given at the Christiania Theatre, January 17, 1864, but was first made famous through the German productions, in 1875, by the excellent *ensemble* of the Duke of Saxe-Meiningen's players. The play is to all appearance historical, built mainly of material contained in "Haakon Haakonsson's Saga." The frequent change of scene, coupled with the "chronicle style," reminds one strongly of Shakespeare's histories. The historic verities, in the main, are kept intact, yet the reconstructive tendency is perceptibly slighter than in *The Vikings*, particularly as regards the linguistic makeup. The reason of this comparative indifference to the temporal flavor is not far to seek. Under guise of the past, Ibsen's real concern is with things and ideas of his own day. The experience with *Love's Comedy* had made him wary of sending his opinions to the joust under their own arms and with visor open. *The Pretenders*, consequently, is the first of Ibsen's "Schlüsseldramen," and in this capacity requires perhaps some "first aid" to the understanding. On the safe authority of George Brandes we have to identify Earl Skule with Ibsen himself, while King Haakon represents Ibsen's more fortunate competitor for leadership, Björnstjerne Björnson. Although doubtless there exists this parallelism, it does not extend to all phases of the drama, for the contestants in the play have their historic function as well, and above all else a self-directing and self-consistent dramatic existence. Their similarity to the two writers lies mainly in the situation, — two men of power contending for the leadership of Norway's people. In portraying their characters, Ibsen has been far more generous to his younger rival than to himself. Haakon figures as a brave and buoyant leader of men, confident of his righteous cause, just and energetic, secure in his kingship because he is endowed by birth and fortune with all kingly qualities. Skule, on the other hand, is a man wrecked in his private happiness and spoiled for chieftaincy by brooding distrust of others and himself. Tormenting doubt of his call was Ibsen's own frame of mind in his harassed and straitened circumstances. He was losing confidence in his poetic vocation

because he was not wholly firm in mind as to the truth of
his own convictions. One passage in the drama especially
throws light on this attitude. Jatgeir the Skald has as-
serted that just as some men need sorrow to become sing-
ers, so others there may be who need faith or joy — or
doubt: —

King Skule. Doubt as well?
Jatgeir. Ay, but then must the doubter be strong and sound.
King Skule. And whom do you call the unsound doubter?
Jatgeir. Him who doubts of his own doubt.[1]

The office of Skule as a personification of the poet's own
tortured state of mind is corroborated by a suite of sonnets, *In the Picture Gallery* ("I billedgaleriet," 1859).[2]
The poet's besetting enemy, Doubt, is pictured as a black
elf prompting him with words of discouragement. Professor Roman Woerner, perhaps the subtlest student of Ibsen,
is, however, right in regarding the victory of Haakon over
Skule as the "description of a saving crisis in a mind that
is full of vital energies." Whatever there was in the poet's
nature of cowardly and abasing elements which had im-
mediately made common cause against him with the ven-
omous calumnies and insults from without, is overcome by
the militant, triumphantly aspiring traits of his character,
and forever expelled.*ʰ* The personal allusion that lies in
the play forms, however, merely an accessory interest. It
does not touch its essential meaning, which lies open to all
the world, not only to those initiated in Ibsen's private
triumphs or grievances. Mr. Haldane Macfall seeks to
epitomize that meaning by a clever contrast: "Here we
have the tragedy of the man who steals the *thought* of an-

---

[1] Vol. II, p. 260.   [2] *SW*ⁱⁱ, vol. I, pp. 257-71.

other — just as in *The Vikings* we have the tragedy of the man who steals the *deed* of another." ' Stated in terms of motives rather than of acts, it is equally true that *The Pretenders* is one of the maturest dramatic treatments of overweening ambition ; the tragedy of a talent which falls short of the highest achievement because of its inherent inadequacy, but which still cannot find happiness on any lower level. At the same time the momentous chapter of the national history here reproduced has a more than individual significance. The drama reveals a prophetic understanding of Norwegian character and destiny. Ibsen's higher intellect had been slowly maturing. With this work it proves itself to have come of age. .

Technically considered, also, *The Pretenders* marks a great stride on the way to perfection. Whereas in *The Vikings* the *dramatis personæ* hardly deviate from the stereotyped literary patterns of vice and virtue unadmixed, we find in *The Pretenders* light and shadow boldly juxtaposed in the abounding humanity of the characters. Magnificently imagined here, too, are the women: Inga, for whom the poet's mother was the model, Margrete, Ingeborg, Ragnhild. Perhaps it is a technical flaw, however, that the interest encompasses two heroes in equal measure, and that a third character rivals both of them in spiritual fascination. For in the same category as one of the great character parts of the modern theatre is the figure of Bishop Nicholas Arnesson. Here we see Ibsen rise to his full stature as a master of portraiture. To the superficial view, Nicholas is merely a singular congeries of evil traits, a species of Shakespeare's Richard III or Schiller's Franz Moor. But on closer examination the complex character

the Government for relief; it was not till 1866 that he obtained from the Storthing the coveted allowance. In the meantime he was glad enough to get, at the solicitation of Björnson and other faithful and influential friends, a traveling purse of four hundred specie dollars, which, eked out by generous private assistance, would enable him to live one year abroad in reasonable security from want.

So in April, 1864, Henrik Ibsen, thirty-six years of age, exiled himself from Norway, and became almost for the whole remainder of his active life that pitiable object among men, a man without a country. Yet there was to come a time when under the still vivid smart of his expulsion he could not suppress a singular feeling of gratitude for that chastening and bracing experience. In 1872 he sent home his *Ode for the Millennial Celebration* ("Ved Tusendaarfesten") of Norway's Union.

My countrymen, who filled for me deep bowls
Of wholesome bitter medicine, such as gave
The poet, on the margin of his grave,
Fresh force to fight where broken twilight rolls, —
My countrymen, who sped me o'er the wave,
An exile, with my griefs for pilgrim-soles,
My fears for burdens, doubts for staff, to roam, —
From the wide world I send you greeting home.

I send you thanks for gifts that help and harden,
Thanks for each hour of purifying pain,
Each plant that springs in my poetic garden
Is rooted where your harshness poured its rain;
Each shoot in which it blooms and burgeons forth
It owes to that gray weather from the North;
The sun relaxes, but the fog secures!
My country, thanks! My life's best gifts were yours.[1]

[1] *Digte,* in *M*, vol. III, pp. 130-35; *SW*, vol. I, pp. 160-66. Cf. Gosse, p. 143, whence the translation is borrowed.

Political events of a momentous nature had added to Ibsen's disgust with his compatriots and superinduced his resolution to quit the country. At the very close of 1863 the so-called second Danish war had broken out on account of the political status of Schleswig-Holstein. The Danes, clutched by the joint superior forces of Prussia and Austria, were ignominiously left in the lurch by their neighbors and brothers of Norway and Sweden. Ibsen never could forgive the Norwegians for not having hastened to the aid of the consanguineous nation. The integrity of Schleswig as a part of Denmark had been a Scandinavian slogan up to the very time of the catastrophe. The breach of faith was the more grievous and inexcusable, as it was not committed by royal incentive, but against the deceased King's wishes by the Storthing representing the people of Norway. "Just as *The Pretenders* appeared, Frederick VII died and the war began. I wrote the poem *A Brother in Distress*.[1] Of course it was without effect against the Norwegian Yankeedom which had beaten me at every point, and so I went into exile." This is Ibsen's own explanation of why he turned his back on his native country. But enough has been said to show that his divorce from Norway came as much from social and economic exigencies as from the clash of his patriotic ardor with the apathy of the people.

Not that his patriotism was then to be doubted. In his works up to, and including, his first masterpiece, *The Pretenders*, the national Norwegian note is clearly, almost stridently, audible. And yet he was not cut out for a popular favorite. In his political and social attitude from his

---

[1] *Digte*, in *M*, vol. III, p. 82 ; *SW*, vol. I, pp. 61–63.

first puerile outbursts in *Catilina*, Ibsen behaves not as a fiery reformer, rather as a malcontent, unable to bear the restraints imposed by association or to submit to the discipline of a party. He thus failed to construct an effective background for his reformatory activity, the political as well as the social. One reason why Norway was not more deeply stirred by the efforts we have contemplated was that these manifestoes seemed to be lacking in the ingratiations of whole-souled enthusiasm. Was Ibsen perhaps too serious to be taken seriously by the masses? People "felt" in his work a "lack of ideals and convictions." How so many came to think of him as only a critic of the destructive sort, too indolent and indifferent to the weal of humanity to lend a hand in the laying of hard and solid foundations for the higher up-stepping of society, is not easy to explain. Of a certainty the subsequent file of his work sdoes not permit a denial of his idealism. They are one and all emanations of noble idealism, albeit their first intent is to touch the vital necessities of our real existence.

CHAPTER IV

BRAND — PEER GYNT

IN curious contradiction to the common opinion that was held about him, Ibsen felt strongly within him the call to be a preacher and a leader of men. His works are of didactical origin, and in so far as they are imperfect, their imperfections lie in that fact. The opposition to him has sought to make capital out of their "tendenciousness," — as though the art of letters stood and fell with Oscar Wilde's finical definition that the sole purpose and meaning of literature is distinction, charm, beauty, and imaginative power. Are we not apt to forget, when deprecating the problem drama of the present, that many great plays of a much earlier day were "Tendenzstücke," no less than *Peer Gynt* and *Pillars of Society?* Schiller's dramas were animated by the strongest ethical motives. No less is this true of Lessing. Nor was the habit ever confined to "pedantic" Germany. Beaumarchais's *Figaro*, Corneille's *Cid* are "plays with a purpose" if ever there were any. Victor Hugo, and a host of younger dramatists before and after Augier and Sardou, would fall under the same æsthetic ban as Ibsen. He simply chanced to be the first poet to build dramas with our *modern* tendencies.[a] A "Tendenzdichter," then, Ibsen was, and without a frank acknowledgment of his plays as instruments of social propaganda no discussion of them could be very profitable. They are not particularly concerned about a consistent theory of

art, however admirable their technical construction. But
as to the tenets of Ibsen's social — or should we say anti-
social? — ethics, these are breathed forth from every page
of his writings. As a moralist, Ibsen was militant, aggres-
sive, contentious. A measure of impatience, nay intolerance, clearly in excess of practical utility for one who
would be a reformer, supplied generous employment for
his fine pugnacity; we may call it fine because it was put in
action for noble causes. For all of Ibsen's work is inspired
and guided, like that of his contemporary Tolstoy, by the
principle of truthfulness. "Dare to be true" — that is
his simple message; only the advice is not addressed to
mankind at large, for Ibsen despises the great majority.
His understanding of character is profound but cynical;
even where he loves, his love is tainted with bitterness.
To his thinking, like Nietzsche's, the throng is doomed
to callousness and stupor; no use trying to improve
and convert the mass; for, as Mr. Shaw avers, the mass
is pure machinery and has no principles except principles of mechanics. A saner thing to do is to further and
direct the needful revolt of the exalted that are worth saving, against the Brummagem morality of the cud-chewing
crowd. The nature of these few and select is essentially
noble, though it has been misled to false standards through
perverse education. As for the inferiority of the average
fellowman, shut your eyes to it, and yours will surely be
the fate of a Brand, a Stockmann, a Gregers Werle, according to the measure and quality of your individual folly.

Brand (1866) came into being, says Ibsen, "as a result
of something which I had not *observed*, but *experienced*." [1]

---

[1] *C*, p. 193; cf. also *C*, p. 190.

He had wrought after the fashion of all true poets from an inward necessity, in order to disburden himself of a painful experience. Since it is the main object of this book to interpret Ibsen's *ideas*, so as to facilitate his recognition as one of the shaping factors of modern culture, we cannot devote so much attention to the artistic aspects of his dramas. Were one speaking primarily of the master of the dramatic craft, there would indeed be very much to say. Not that there is any intention of entirely overlooking Ibsen's technical service. Right here it is well to insist that his dramas, while replete with intellectual intention, are not tracts but works of art. To this a special reminder should be added anent *Brand*, that it is not to be appraised as a drama, even though it is such in name, but — much as *Faust* or some of Browning's best products — as a "dramatic poem." Although it has eventually reached the theatre, it was not conceptually designed for the stage.[1] It is the first work Ibsen created at a distance from home. He wrote it in 1865, for the most part at Ariccia, near Rome, in the summer months, during which it was his wont to cast his work into a final shape. It was written in riming lines, of four stresses each, changing irregularly from the iambic to the trochaic genus of rhythm. The lilt and melody of the verse had not a little to do with the immense public response. So unexpectedly great was this that within less than four months three good-sized editions were exhausted. To this rousing success no small part was contributed by the circumstance that through

---

[1] In fact it was first conceived as an epic. The epic *Brand* fragments are to be found in *SW*[II], vol. II, pp. 93–154; the very scholarly introduction by Karl Larsen, pp. 47–91, throws much light on the composition.

his friend Björnson's intercession Ibsen's writings, beginning with *Brand,* were published by Frederik Hegel
(Gyldendalske Bokhandel) of Copenhagen, justly called
the Cotta of the North.

Ibsen used to warn his visitors and correspondents
against searching for specific "teachings" in his plays.
But this does not alter the undeniable fact that a thesis
or contention of some sort is expounded in each of his
works, barring possibly the sole instance of *Hedda Gabler.*
The *hæc fabula docet* is never absent from his satires. In
this didactical temper of the poet lies also the explanation of his ineradicable bias for symbolism and allegory.
The truth-seeking realist in Ibsen, however, always
sends the sermonizer looking for his models in the province of the actual. Realistic, too, as a rule, is the background in these pictures. In *Brand,* needless to repeat,
that background is political or, better, historical; the
fiery harangues of the hero have a barbed point for the
Norwegian conscience, for they make the people recollect
with what criminal indifference they had looked on the
de-Scandinavization of Schleswig-Holstein after the vo-
luminous rhetoric expended at their mass meetings.

But who was the original Brand? With much likelihood
of truth Sören Kierkegaard (1813-1855)[b] has been suggested; and in spite of Ibsen's express denial that remarkable man's life and doctrine, in particular his religious
rigor which led to his violent separation from his church
and to a tragic ending, left unquestionable marks of influence in the great poem.

In Kierkegaard theologian and philosopher were
blended. He devoted his meditations almost entirely to

the subject of religion, but his interest attached not to the
details of dogma, but to the basic principle of Christianity. This he interpreted in a spirit different from that of
other religious leaders in that he upheld with the utmost
emphasis and consistency the "absolute ideal demand,"
resembling, in this respect, the contemporary German radical thinker Ludwig Feuerbach (1804–1872). Yet the two
thinkers arrive from similar premises at far-sundered poles
of belief: Feuerbach renouncing Christianity, while Kierkegaard embraced it with ever-growing fervor. In his conception the Christian religion is, objectively viewed, para-
doxical and absurd, and repellent to the reason or the
"common sense"; it attains reality and validity solely in
the *religious consciousness*, and becomes an object of passionate love for the believer. Life in the faith, he claims,
is a contract between the Divinity and the individual.
For congregational religious practice he has a pronounced
distaste. The "official" Christianity of the churches was
vehemently condemned by Kierkegaard on the ground of
its aversion, nay outright opposition, to the imitation of
Christ. Christianity as it exists to-day he maintained to
be a partnership between Christ's teaching and a worldly
doctrine, a partnership from which the nobler member is
gradually pushed and crowded out. Real Christianity is
equivalent to renunciation of the world. Hence the religion of Christ should and must be a gospel of sorrow.
Kierkegaard's powerful influence was due in large measure
to his noble, uplifting diction and delivery.[c] However, the
personality of Brand is drawn in some of its essentials
after one of Kierkegaard's disciples with whom Ibsen was
acquainted at home and afterwards in Dresden, the

evangelist Gustav Adolph Lammers (1802–1878); so Ibsen
stated to his biographer Henrik Jaeger. Lammers, who
was a pastor in Ibsen's native town of Skien, played a
prominent part in the revolt against the established
church. His agitation reached a climax in 1855, the same
year as Kierkegaard's, and led to his resignation from the
pastorate. In 1856 he founded a free congregation that
worshiped in the fields and on the hills under the open sky,
— in *Brand* poetic use of the incident is made. But over
and above these relations to other men, Brand is also a
self-portrait of the poet, as are other leading figures in his
plays, reflecting the deep impressions of spiritual experiences recently passed through. At all events, Brand must
be classed as a composite portrait, not a strictly true copy
from life. While upon the subject of resemblances, the
similarity of *Brand* to Gerhart Hauptmann's fairy drama,
The Sunken Bell (1897), may be pointed out. It extends
beyond the central *motif* to many features of composition
and characterization. Agnes, the wife, as well as Brand
himself, and their philistine *entourage*, also entire scenes,
like the exodus to the mountains, have their counterpart
in the much later work of the German poet.

George Brandes has aptly characterized *Brand* as the
"tragedy of idealism." One might with equal justice
call it the tragedy of the extremist. The incompatibility
of the practical and the ideal had been revealed before,
though more timorously, in *Love's Comedy*. In *Brand* the
subject receives drastic treatment. Brusquely a challenge was here hurled against the vapid pietism of the
Norwegian people; their half-souled enthusiasm and re-
luctance to follow their own ideals. To Ibsen, for the first

time in the history of his land, fell the stern duty of the
patriot to chastise and chasten his fatherland. There is
perhaps no truer test of patriotism.

He flouts the cardinal national faults under the simile
of the three evil genii —

> Which wildest reel, which blindest grope,
> Which furthest roam from home and hope: —
> *Light-heart*, who, crown'd with leafage gay,
> Loves by the dizziest verge to play; —
> *Faint-heart*, who marches slack and slow
> Because old wont will have it so;
> *Wild-heart*, who, borne on lawless wings,
> Sees fairness in the foulest things.[1]

But the application of the satire does not have to halt
before the sixty-fifth degree of northern latitude. It
would be extremely unfair for Europeans, or Americans
for the matter of that, to read out of *Brand* an exclusive
indictment of the brave little northern nation. On the
issues raised, all nations are equally at sea, and nearly all
in the same boat, and there is no country under this twen-
tieth-century sun where it is made more difficult than with
us for the "differenced" man, the "Adelejer" in the sense
of Ibsen, to save his selfhood for the efficient performance of a part in the economy of society.

> We stand on democratic ground,
> Where what the people think is right;
> Shall one against the mass propound
> His special views on black and white?[2]

Woe to the man who pushes his head above the common
level! Democracy insists relentlessly on conformance to

---

[1] Vol. III, p. 36. The passages from *Brand* are given in the rendering
by Professor C. H. Herford. *Brand* has also been translated by William Archer. Both translations are preceded by valuable introductions.

[2] Vol. III, p. 140.

its ideals. So it makes for a dead level and insures the rule
of the commonplace. It standardizes men, uniforms them
sartorially, morally, and intellectually. According to the
prevailing gospel of mediocrity the eleventh commandment reads: Be like unto one another. Do not grow beyond the average measure.

> Let each his own excrescence pare,
> Neither uplift him, nor protrude,
> But vanish in the multitude.[1]

and: —

> But all your angles must be rounded,
> Your gnarls and bosses scraped and pounded!
> You must grow sleek as others do,
> All singularities eschew,
> If you would labor without let.[2]

What is unfailingly the result, if this principle is applied
beyond a certain medium level of civilization? Ibsen answers for us: "The very praiseworthy attempt to make
our people a democratic community has inadvertently
gone a good way toward making us a plebeian community." [3]

The fear of being dissonant with the rest of the world
causes men to seek refuge in the relinquishment of the central ego, and results ultimately in the loss of personality,
the abandonment of the very essence of life.

> *The Sexton.* But yet you said that life was best?
> *The Schoolmaster.* By dean and deacon that's professed.
> And I too, say so, like the rest, —
> Provided, mind, the "life" in view
> Is that of the great Residue.[4]

The fight with fortune can be won only in alliance
with public opinion: hence man is softened, to use an

[1] Vol. III, p. 207.　[2] *Ibid.*, p. 208.　[3] *C*, p. 351.　[4] Vol. III, p. 180.

Emersonian phrase, into a "mush of concession." True
manhood is effectually neutralized by the chief organs of
the body politic. Church and State side with the mean-
natured. The collision between the single will and the
many-headed is most unequal.

> *The Schoolmaster.* We cannot fitly condescend
> To smirch ourselves in human slime.
> Let no man, says the Parson, dare
> To be two things at the same time;
> And with the best will, no one can
> Be an official and a man.[1]

In the terror of public opinion lies deeply rooted the
universal evil of hypocrisy, the first concomitant of sordid
selfishness. Ibsen, like his Brand, feels keenly that society
works sinfully against its vital interest when it ruthlessly
irons out the inherent human tendency to variation from
the type. Two generations ago Darwin, endowing the
world with a new organon in the science of evolution,
taught the high bio-economic value of differentiation.
Yet seemingly the truth has not even now percolated our
dense social intelligence that, so far from being contrary
to the law of nature, social differentiation is actually en-
joined upon humankind. In his illuminating collection
of lectures, *The Bible of Nature*, Professor J. Arthur
Thomson points out a noteworthy lesson concerning the
preciousness of individuality.

Variations supply the raw material of progress, and variations spell individuality. This is one of the biological common-
places which in human affairs we persistently ignore. In the
educational mill . . . and in our inexorable social criticism,
how systematically we pick off the buds of individuality, —

[1] Vol. III, p. 186.

idiosyncrasies and crankiness, we say, — spoiling how many flowers. It is said that we do this to prevent failures and criminals, but are we very successful in this prevention? How many of both do we make by repressing individuality? [d]

Modern opposition to the philistinism of society, its resemblance to a centrifugal dissipation of force notwithstanding, is ulteriorly the last remove from an anti-social crusade. It springs in reality from a scientific basis. The antidotes and cure-alls prescribed for the social disease of stagnancy are apt perhaps to be worse than the disease. Or how much comfort is there to be derived for the ills we bear from the thought of Nietzsche's "gorgeous blonde roving beast" amuck midst social chaos? Seldom have philosophical inferences been more conflicting than in the interpretation of Ibsen's social gospel. But no sympathetic student of Ibsen will refuse to join in the verdict that his social ideas and ideals do not exceed the bounds of reason and legitimate expectation of the future. At heart never a red-hot revolutionist, his at first excessive individualism passes step by step into a generous, yet prudent subjectivism which aims to vindicate full freedom for the individual, without fatally ignoring, after the extremist's fashion, the eternal principles of justice and righteousness. Everybody should be encouraged to rise, even though but few will gain the crest of the mountain.

Let us stop at this point of our study to inquire for Ibsen's social creed and doctrine at the time when with *Brand* he came prominently before the public. We must not forget, however, that his socio-critical tenets underwent, in the course of his moral and mental evolution, some extremely significant modifications. But since it so happens that Americans identify Ibsen's convictions mainly with the gist of his earlier works, let us for the present be content to indicate the general drift of his social philosophy during what may be termed his anarchistical period. The relation of his theories to the spirit of the times, to which they are in sharp opposition, is perfectly obvious.

It was essentially an era of political reconstruction that preceded and followed the great Franco-Prussian War.[6] The fast-growing popular consciousness demanded of the constituted authorities a bettering of material conditions and likewise an extension of liberties. The governments, at least those of Germany, feeling securer than ever in their greatly strengthened prestige, made no haste to fulfill the liberal demands. From this resulted a strenuous activity among the Liberals to obtain relief through the one obviously legitimate channel. They set about in earnest to reform the organized institutions. To Ibsen, with his undemocratic, in fact outright anti-democratic notions, that idea was repugnant. To his view, the endeavors of the political reformers had an altogether wrong aim. He frankly tells us that "changes in forms of government are mere pettifogging affairs," denoting a degree less or a degree more of foolishness. Even total revolutions in the controlling agencies of society would be unable to set the world right. Nothing can do that, thinks the author of *Catilina* and *Love's Comedy*, save a radical self-effectuation of society along lines of unrestricted freedom. Ibsen, then, dreams, like many a Utopian before him and after him, of a development of the individual so wonderful in its efficacy and reach that under enlightened anarchy mankind would attain an almost ideal state. We should note broadly at the outset that, inasmuch as his Utopia postulates the complete regeneration of man, it would be preposterous to call Ibsen a pessimist.

What is there in the way of that happy re-birth? No smaller obstacle than society itself and its chief agent, the state. Ibsen in his early ardor did not scruple to enunciate the consequences. In letters to Brandes written in 1870–1871, he exasperatedly inveighs against the state. "Away with the state," shouts he; "I will take part in that revolution."[1] He makes the bold assertion that the duty of the higher personality is to undermine every form of government. And this idea, with its dangerous correlates, becomes for a short while a veritable obsession with him. But the excesses of the French Commune opened his eyes and made him relinquish his faith in the unmixed desirability of lawless blessedness. Finding himself forced to repudiate the gospel of lawlessness as a thing for which mankind is not quite ready, he nevertheless continues radical in thought and attitude. He pleads now for relative liberty: since absolute freedom is impracticable, let the individual enjoy the largest amount of freedom that is possible. This might strike us but as a circuitous plea for the conservation of the existing order, if Ibsen did not continue to denounce the existing order and its regnant code of morals. The truth of the matter is, Ibsen cared next to nothing for liberty in the usual party sense of the word. "Liberty," he once said, "is not the same thing as political liberty." The following might have come from the pen of Lessing, so strikingly alike is it in tone and

[1] *C*, p. 208.

feeling to that famous passage in the latter's reply to Head-Pastor Goeze: "The only thing I love about liberty is the struggle for it. I care nothing for the possession of it. He who possesses liberty otherwise than as an aspiration, possesses it dead and soulless." But Ibsen ends with a malicious thrust: " It is, however, exactly this dead maintenance of a certain given standpoint of liberty that is characteristic of the communities which go by the name of states — and this is what I have called worthless."[1] Only an idealist could utter such words, and who could be farther removed from pessimism than an idealist with a faith in the progressive evolution of human ideals! At a banquet in 1887, Ibsen said: "I believe that the biologic theory of evolution is true also regarding spiritual phases of life. . . . I have repeatedly been called a pessimist. And so I am, in so far as I disbelieve in the constancy of human ideals. But I am likewise an optimist, in so far as I firmly believe in the self-procreation of ideals and in their capacity of development."[2] Ibsen is not a pessimist, for he does not think life an evil, but an *optimist*, because he thinks life too good to be wasted as we waste it. Both idealism and individualism enter into Ibsen's peremptory command: "*Be yourself.*" The test of selfhood, however, lies in the willingness to suffer for one's ideals. I sometimes wonder why those who in spite of everything insist on calling Ibsen a pessimist do not change the indictment and call him, on the contrary, "überspannt" or "verstiegen." They would be excusable on the ground of his idealism being incomprehensible to meaner natures.

Ibsen's social panacea, we have said, is truthfulness. As

[1] *C*, p. 208.　　　　[2] *SNL*, p. 57.

poet, thinker, and social critic he dedicates himself to
the service of Truth. By truthfulness, he means loyalty
and fidelity to one's self. Maintenance of selfhood is the
foremost duty. Man should take no dictates from without.
The measure and motive power of his conduct should pro-
ceed from within. He should do what his will prompts
him to do. Only in this case can he be called a personality.
In *Brand* the thought is forcibly expressed in the temer-
arious challenge: —

> Be passion's slave, be pleasure's thrall, —
> But be it utterly, all in all!
> Be not to-day, to-morrow one,
> Another when a year is gone.
> Be what you are with all your heart,
> And not by pieces and in part.[1]

To fulfill one's self — therein should man seek his mission,
as it is his right.

> Room within the wide world's span
> Self completely to fulfill,
> That's a valid right of man,
> And no more than that I will.[2]

Ibsen's greatest dread, — we may say his one great
dread, — and his most constant theme upon which he
plays so many variations, is the lie. The conduct he sanc-
tions consists negatively in abstention from every form
of falsehood, positively in the vigorous assertion of true
convictions and war of extermination waged regardless of
consequences against all recognized wrongs and shams.
Now, in a world ruled by cant and compromise, the
hebdomadal bit of meek official admonishment from the
pulpit can do no appreciable good.

[1] Vol. III, p. 22.　　　　　　[2] *Ibid.*, p. 61.

istics. For the poet plainly intended that the worthless fellow, too, should have his redeeming traits. At all events, there resulted a rupture between Norway's two greatest sons. It was patched up for the time being, but soon after that Ibsen gave genuine ground for offense by referring to Björnson in a mordant poem entitled *Nordens Signaler* ("The Northern Signals," 1872)[1] as a political weather-cock, because Björnson had urged Denmark to forget about Schleswig and reconcile herself with Germany.[a]

Stensgaard, the central butt of the satire, is a soul steeped in the Gyntian sort of mendacity; the kind that intoxicates himself with his own vaporings and transiently swindles himself into believing his own phrenetic declamations, like Armado in *Love's Labor's Lost*, a man

> That hath a mint of phrases in his brain;
> One whom the music of his own vain tongue
> Doth ravish like enchanting harmony.

Not such a very bad fellow fundamentally, but thoroughly spoiled for good honest work by his spouting eloquence, among other causes. He possesses that elusive quality of "magnetism," which in only too many cases issues from brazen and rock-ribbed self-assurance. On this intangible asset he stakes his claim to a public career, and becomes, like hundreds of other ambitious orators, a cheap, hollow charlatan and political trimmer. One moment the ferocious demagogue, the next moment the champion of the established order. One moment the big brother of the poor, the next moment the little brother of the rich. "Woe to him," once exclaimed Henrik Ibsen, "who has to think of his parents with aversion!" Stensgaard bears a hered-

[1] *SW*, vol. I, pp. 276-78.

itary taint, albeit of a different order from that of Dr. Rank, Brand, Gynt, Oswald, Rebecca, etc. His is a servile and venal nature, to be had for any sop thrown to his ambition. A dinner invitation from the local magnate overthrows his radical convictions. His life, even in its most sacred privacies, is to be ordered with a single eye to profit and preferment; marriage is to serve him as a lever to wealth, station, and influence; accordingly a single glance into a luxurious household determines him to marry the daughter. By the irony of fate, and not perchance by the eternal fitness of things, the ardent pretender to popularity and favor manages to fall down midways between the several chairs of ease which he has put in place for himself. His pitiable undoing is not meant as a blazing judgment against unrighteousness, but simply goes to show that Stensgaard is as yet too green to beat in the game of politics. Many an aspiring politician felt himself hit by the reverberating shot Ibsen had fired. A tempest of indignation and ill-will broke over the performance of the play in Christiania. And so this capital comedy, which by its dash and go and irresistible merriment completely refutes the inveterate superstition that Ibsen lacked humor (as though without this precious possession he could have had so much sympathy with the wrongs and foibles of men!) missed its highly deserved success. But even had the response been different, Ibsen would not have been influenced in the choice of his further course. The sphere of strictly political comedy would in any case have proved too narrow for his genius, already bound for the much wider sphere of the social drama.

The League of Youth is technically far in advance of its
author's previous efforts. So far as the structural qualities
go, the almost inextricable tangle of mistakes, misunder-
standings, and surprises attests the still prevalent influence of Scribe. By marked contrast to the more or less
conventional comicry of the situations the originality of
the coming technique announces itself. The realistic
method of presentment evolved by conscientious experiment is now for the first time in Ibsen's grasp. The action
is managed without monologues and without a single
occurrence of the "aside" and the "stage-whisper." The
dialogue is in prose and follows much the natural mode of
conversation. To us, such features in drama offer not
the least matter for surprise; but upon the audience of
1869, sufficiently enraged by the satirical intent of the
play, the daring formal innovation produced an effect like
an extra insult thrown in with the injury.

After an uncommonly prolonged incubation, the
"world-tragedy" *Emperor and Galilean* ("Kejser og Gal-
ilæer," 1873) was finished.[1] The theme, as has been mentioned, had stirred the poet ever since his arrival in Italy.[c]
Already in 1864 he prepared to write a tragedy on the
Apostate.[2] The subject was taken up again in 1866, casu-
ally, and more vigorously once more in 1870, while Ibsen
resided at Dresden. It was planned (till 1872) to be a trilogy[3] consisting of (1) *Julian and the Philosophers* (in three
acts), (2) *Julian's Apostasy* (in three acts), (3) *Julian on
the Imperial Throne* (in five acts). Eventually the bulky

---

[1] On the genesis and completion of *Emperor and Galilean*, cf. *C*, pp.
117, 121, 185, 206, 215, 222, 236, 239, 245, 249–50, 267, 269, 280.
    [2] *C*, p. 78.   [3] *C*, pp. 236 and particularly 243.

material was compressed into two parts of five acts each,
Part First, *Cæsar's Apostasy* ("Cæsars Frafald"), Part
Second, *The Emperor Julian* ("Kejser Julian").

In Ibsen's own estimation — yet great men are fallible
in appraising their own achievements — this was the greatest of all his works. By it he meant to confute those critics
who denied to him a "positive" world-view, as many are
doing with too much emphasis to this day. For this purpose the drama was to body forth a doctrine. A dramatist's right to externalize his philosophy in any fit form
may pass unchallenged. Yet there is no getting beyond
the critical questions, Is the philosophy wholly inwoven in
the action, incarnate in the persons? Does it shine forth
from the characters, or does it only shimmer and flicker
through them from an outer source of light? Ibsen speaks
with fair assurance on the subject. "There is in the character of Julian, as in most that I have written during my
riper years, more of my own spiritual experience than I
care to acknowledge to the public. But it is at the same
time an entirely realistic piece of work. The figures stood
solidly before my eyes in the light of their time — and I
hope they will so stand before the reader's eyes." [1]

Intent on putting the greatest possible amount of
truthfulness into the portrayal of Græco-Roman life,
he expended for once a vast deal of painstaking, minute
study. Nevertheless the great drama cannot be said to
be historically truthful, save as to exteriors and inci-
dentals. The figure of the protagonist is decidedly mis-
drawn. Ibsen would have done well to abide by the
verdict of the historian Negri, who pronounced Julian

[1] *C*, p. 255.

"a Puritan in the purple, morally too Christian to be a Christian of the fourth century church." Ibsen treated the character of Julian with willful injustice, portraying him as a monstrously conceited degenerate, without sense, balance, or even the semblance of royal dignity. This raving Cæsaro-maniac seems more fit for a Punch and Judy show than for a "world-tragedy," as Ibsen termed his drama. An oddly compounded dilettante[1] is this Julian, seemingly playing a burlesque on the historic emperor.[2] The latter perished as the victim of the final contest between two moral constitutions battling in his soul for the dominion of the future. That, too, was Ibsen's view of his hero, but what he brought forth was the sheer miscarriage of a grand poetical conception. To tell the truth, the playwright had undertaken what lay outside the province of his craft. As a rule his persons are firmly established in their character. Brandes says rightly that the action only serves to test and prove the immutability of the *dramatis personæ*. (Only it should be added to this estimate that we do not see all their potentialities at the first glance.) Now in *Emperor and Galilean* the attempt is made to trace the gradual transformation of the entire character of the hero: an attempt that ended in dismal failure. For the character does not progress and develop, but perpetually flutters and flounders. Julian is utterly without a directing self-consciousness. Everlastingly boggling over the freedom of his will, he is withal grossly superstitious. Caught in the mesh of events, he would

[1] Especially in his philosophical divagations throughout both parts of the tragedy.

[2] Notably in Part II, Act II, Sc. 1.

propitiate the gods, pray and sacrifice to them. "To what gods? I will sacrifice to this God and that God — one or the other must surely hear me. I *must* call on something without me and above me."[1] In his habitual state of confusion he becomes a chronic client of the oracles. When they withhold their counsel, he becomes despondent and whines: "To stand so entirely alone!" Like Peer Gynt he strives after his own satisfaction, seeks to be "enough to himself." Since in drama there can be no hero without the potentiality of deeds, Julian is utterly unsuited to his task. He excites our curiosity and pity, but even the outcry wrung from him at his final collapse, that historic admission, "Thou hast conquered, Galilean," comes too late to save him our respect.

Emperor and Galilean stands in a patent dialectic relation to *Brand* and *Peer Gynt*. Together they form a species of psychological trilogy. Unavoidably we are driven to employ the Hegelian notation in pointing out this inner connectedness. *Brand*, then, stands for the "thesis," here carried to the point of self-contradiction which any single idea will reach if pursued to its fullest lengths. In *Peer Gynt* the antithesis is sharply stated; in *Emperor and Galilean* the opposition of the positive and the negative poles of truth is succeeded by the higher synthesis of truth. This process of reasoning, Hegel designates as the "Trichotomy." Characteristically for Ibsen's philosophical allegiance the tripartite logic pervades also *Emperor and Galilean* by itself, outside of any association with other plays. This drama, Ibsen confessed, was not the first he had written in Germany, but indeed the first he wrote

[1] Vol. v, p. 458.

under the influence of German intellectual life.[1] The special philosophical theme of *Emperor and Galilean*, as over against *Brand* and *Peer Gynt*, to put it with extreme conciseness, is the freedom of will. In all probability Ibsen culled the main conceptions from Schopenhauer, but he lent them new emotional values.

The philosophical foundation of Ibsen's "world-drama" is, moreover, almost identical with the metaphysics underlying the work of his great predecessor in the practical reform of the drama, Friedrich Hebbel (1813–1863). Both poets postulate the regnancy supreme and absolute of a "Weltwille," a will inherent in the universe. On the philosophical plane of *Emperor and Galilean*, Ibsen, like Hebbel, attributes to the world an intelligent self-direction. Judged, then, from a posited consciousness of our union with the world-will, events must be regarded by us not as the haphazards of blind fate, but rather as volitional acts of the universal Ego. But the volitional freedom of the world's self-consciousness, translated into individual conduct, spells necessity. Now, inasmuch as the progress and betterment of the world is achieved through the instrumentality of men with a strong "will,"—both Hebbel and Ibsen, the latter in particular, are hero-worshipers, — this philosophy would seem to lead into a dilemma: we are unfree, as to our will, yet freedom of will is our criterion of worth. The contradiction here in the conception of the heroic personality as a man of action, yet not a free agent, is, of course, not confined to drama, but founded in life itself. The only escape from the dilemma lies in the belief that nature implants the power of will in men in order to

[1] *C*, p. 413; *SNL*, p. 109.

bend it to her own, often recondite, means. An individual rebelling against the will of the world is none the less fulfilling an assigned task. He does not choose to do but what a superior power compels him to choose. Mr. Shaw, in his *Quintessence of Ibsenism*, obfuscates what has been called the "Pantragism" of this philosophy[d] by the following comment: "It was something for Julian to have seen that the power which he found stronger than his individual will was itself will; but inasmuch as he conceived it, not as the whole of which his will was but a part, but as a rival will, he was not the man to found the Third Empire."

"What is the way of freedom?" asks the eager Julian.[1] "The God-Emperor or Emperor-God," declares Maximus the Sage, "comes into being in the man *who wills himself*."[2] He who wills, conquers. Yet the parting words are, "To will is to have to will,"[3] and, "I believe in free necessity." Nature makes us will precisely what she wants of us. Accordingly, the tragic hero is invariably in the right, world-philosophically considered. And the beyond-good-and-evil position is reached from a totally different intellectual springboard from that from which Nietzsche took the leap; as when Maximus declares, "Sin lies only in thy sense of sinfulness."[4] Here we have another proof, if one were needed, that the Overman was born into the world of thought a long time before the hermit of Sils-Maria proclaimed him. In Ibsen he is prefigured almost from the earliest dramatic attempts.[5] This, however, it is worth while to remember: Ibsen's "Third Empire," of which

---

[1] Vol. v, p. 112. [2] *Ibid.*, p. 374. [3] *Ibid.*, p. 479. [4] *Ibid.*, p. 108.
[5] Cf. the comment on Bishop Nicholas Arnesson, pp. 51-52.

there is so much question in *Emperor and Galilean*, is, essentially a collectivist, not individualist, Utopia.

Hebbel used a very telling phrase for the infinitely recurring, self-wrecking revolt of the individual against the will of the world; viewing the spectacle as a progressive experiment in education *per contra*, he describes it as the "Selbstkorrektur" of the world, meaning its continuous experimental self-improvement. This concept is also wrought into Nietzsche's philosophy. In his famous theory of the "Wiederkunft des Gleichen" ("Eternal Recurrence")[e] there reëmerges the same notion which we find stated in the second part of *Emperor and Galilean* by the philosopher Maximus: "There is one who ever reappears at certain intervals, in the course of human history. He is like a rider taming a wild horse in the arena. Again and yet again it throws him. A moment, and he is in the saddle again, each time more secure and more expert; but off he has had to go, in all his varying incarnations, until this day. Off he had to go as the God-created man in Eden's grove; off he had to go as the founder of the world-empire; off he must go as the prince of the empire of God. Who knows how often he has wandered among us when none have recognized him? How know you, Julian, that you were not in him whom you now persecute?"[1] Hebbel and Ibsen coincide in the opinion that the march of civilization is regulated by the needs of the times and the preparedness of the people. Yet the levers of progress are the great personalities. Without them we have either stagnation or a stunted, one-sided civilization.

There is no help for our dwelling still further on the

[1] Vol. v, p. 393.

philosophical thought of the double drama, but fortunately it is possible to indicate its drift by uncommented quotation.

Thus speaks Julian among the philosophers: "You know only two streets in Athens, the street to the schools, and the street to the Church; of the third street, toward Eleusis and further, you know naught."[1] In this metaphor, the street to the schools signifies paganism, the street to the Church, Christianity. What is meant by the "street toward Eleusis"? The philosopher Maximus, who kindles in Julian's soul the conflict between the worship of God and self-deification, prophesies a golden age. He confidently predicts the crumbling of the two empires that have gone before; the classic and the romantic world-conception, as we may call them, will be superseded by a new world-ruling religion which shall rear its nobler structure on the ruins of both the old. Three empires were to have sway in their turn. "First that empire which was founded on the tree of knowledge; then that which was founded on the tree of the cross. The third is the empire of the great mystery; that empire which shall be founded on the tree of knowledge and the tree of the cross together, because it hates and loves them both, and because it has its living sources under Adam's grove and under Golgotha."[2] Again, Stirner's and Nietzsche's "gay science" is forestalled: "Where is God? In Olympus? On the cross?" Maximus answers, "No: in my own self. The third empire belongs to him who *wills*." Clearly the poet agreed with Lessing's estimate of the "revealed" religions as so many instruments for the gradual "Education of

[1] Vol. v, pp. 106-07.   [2] *Ibid.*, p. 114.

the Human Race," each being in keeping with its require-
ments for the time being. The "Third Empire" can be
ushered in only by a race developed beyond the present
status of humanity. Only then can the contrast between
pagan Beauty and Christian Truth be resolved in a
higher unity. Neither Julian nor his generation was ripe
for this final synthesis of Truth and Beauty. Julian's palpable mission was to regenerate Christianity as he found
it. He permitted, instead, his deep disappointment in the
Church to grow into hatred of the religion. Then step by
step he advanced in the belief that he himself, not the
Galilean, was God. His relapse from Christianity is conceived as a crime against humanity, whose natural progress was greatly retarded by such retrogression. His was
the power and opportunity of ushering in the "Third
Empire"; — he spurned and repudiated his mission and
wrought tragic mischief in the world. This explains why
Ibsen attributed a world-historic importance to Julian's
apostasy from the Faith. In this spirit Maximus chides
the Apostate. "You have striven to make the youth a
child again. The empire of the flesh is swallowed up in the
empire of the spirit. But the empire of the spirit is not
final, any more than the youth is. You have striven to
hinder the growth of youth — to hinder him from becoming a man. Oh, fool, who have drawn your sword against
that which is to be — against the third empire, in which
the twin-natured shall reign." [1]

Emperor and Galilean met with no enthusiastic reception either from the critics or the public.[9] Ibsen's *opus
maximum*, as he believed it to be, it certainly is not. In

[1] Vol. v, p. 372.

project it was his most ambitious enterprise, in execution
it is perhaps the weakest among all the works of his rip-
ened experience. Its obvious faults are these: It is too
long-drawn-out, especially in the second part. The poet
himself, as a consequence, betrayed his weariness of the
task. It appeals mainly to the intellect, and yet its meaning dives frequently into obscurity.[h] And the characters
are not sufficiently vitalized, so that we are taken aback
both by their inconsistencies and their self-contradictions.
Most serious of all, a cloud of mysticism hangs over the
events, — reality is constantly melting into allegory, as
was already the case to a minor degree in *Brand* and *Peer
Gynt*. In a technical respect also the play is unsuited to
the stage. In the second part there occur no less than
eighteen scenic changes, many of which are uncalled for.
But with all its shortcomings and blemishes, *Emperor and
Galilean* is a solid and noble component in the structure
of the modern drama on which the master builder was
energetically at work. By this time the foundations were
laid, and the walls of the building were rising. Already
it was possible to estimate the area covered, but the
future height of the edifice could not easily be guessed.

CHAPTER VI

THE POET AS MORALIST

A NEW phase of artistic growth and development confronts us now as we pass from the romantic-historical dramas of Ibsen to the stately series of his sociological plays, — we may fitly call them so, — opening with *Pillars of Society*.

After *Brand*, Ibsen's literary position was firmly grounded, so far as Scandinavia was concerned. At that time, however, there was no thought of his subsequent significance for the social, moral, and artistic progress of his age. The period up to his removal from Norway appears in retrospect as one of initiation and apprenticeship. The theatres of Bergen and Christiania were the workshops where he obtained facility in wielding the tools of his craft. The following dozen years developed his art to its full maturity.

His fame was spreading through Europe. George Brandes had probably been the first critic to devote a whole essay to Ibsen's work.ᵃ England and Germany made his acquaintance in the same year, 1872. Mr. Edmund Gosse introduced him to the English, through the offices of the *Spectator*. In Germany a commercial traveler named P. F. Siebold did his best, through articles and translations, to make Ibsen widely known. Adolf Strodtmann (1829–1879) translated *The Pretenders* and *The League of Youth* (both in 1872). The first play done into

English was *Emperor and Galilean* (1876), by Katherine
Ray. In the same year the celebrated players of the Duke
of Saxe-Meiningen produced *The Pretenders* and *The
Vikings*. Yet these conquests were small, foreshowing in
nothing the prodigious influence and vogue of Ibsen in
Germany, which dates from the year 1877. In that year
he launched a practically new form of drama, which met
with instant recognition from many progressive-minded
persons, especially from the brilliant trio, Julius Hoffory,
a Dane by birth, lecturer in the University of Berlin, and
Otto Brahm and Paul Schlenther, conspicuous leaders
then and to-day in the reform of the drama. They became sponsors for Ibsen in Germany just as the actor-
manager, Lugné-Poë (husband of the great actress Su-
zanne Desprès), Count Moriz Prozor, and Mr. André
Antoine, organizer of the Théâtre Libre, made him popular in France. From this time on he advanced step by
step, through the most conscientious exercise of his gifts,
to the undisputed position of the chief dramatist of his age
and one of the greatest of all time. Beside the plays which
he produced from 1877 to about 1900, most of the earlier
plays dwindle into obscure insignificance. Ibsen illustrates
as few other poets do the practical value of hard study.

We must remember that the social problem plays were
begun when the poet was nearing his fiftieth year. His
genius began its highest climb at an age when all other
great dramatists had passed their summit of excellence.
He brought to the task not only the ripeness of experience,
force, and power, but an astonishing capacity for further
growth. In an address made September 10, 1874, to an
audience of enthusiastic university students, he delivered

the lesson of his prolonged apprenticeship by dealing thus
with the crucial question, What is Poetry? "Not till
late in life have my eyes been opened to the fact that to
be a poet means as much as to be a seer; but, mark well,
to see in such a way that the things seen are shown to the
public as the poet has seen them. Now it is a fact that
only those things can be thus seen and assimilated which
are a part of our experience. And this experience is the
secret of modern poetry. All I have written during the
past decade is part of my spiritual experience." [1] And
this further observation explains perhaps adequately his
ultimate conquest of public favor: "No writer makes his
experience alone. Whatever he has perceived in life, his
countrymen have likewise perceived." [2] By these words
Ibsen's priority in many of the opinions whose author he
is reputed to have been is inferentially disclaimed. A
great writer need not be an "original" thinker. His pri-
mary social service and intellectual mission is to articulate
the thought and spirit of his time, not necessarily to
evolve it. Perhaps none of the ideas promulgated in the
works of Henrik Ibsen are, strictly speaking, original with
him. They are the floating notions of an age, caught while
yet invisible or indistinct to the mass of men, and made
palpable by a creative touch. In Ibsen the leading tendencies of the new age became collectively conscious of
themselves. He had the rare courage to state their meaning with fullest force. Such constitutes the social importance of Henrik Ibsen's writings.

Does it not seem incongruous that this hardened re-
cluse, who used to frighten away bold visitors with a

[1] *SW*, vol. i, p. 522; *SNL*, pp. 49-50.   [2] *Ibid.*

venience. Their obsolescence is disguised and they are made to look as good as new, unless, indeed, their very antiqueness adds to their value in the market another element, like threadbare places in an Oriental rug. All moral commandments, not excepting a fraction of the very Decalogue, have thus been tinkered and tampered with. Doctrines are attenuated by sophistry. As a result they are rendered conveniently ambiguous and much less binding, since rules of conduct that are not perfectly intelligible either need not or actually cannot be practiced.ᶜ In consequence of this, society is left without any firm ethical guidance. The old coins have lost their faces, and are no better than mere "counters" in the game. We discredit the old appraisements, yet continue to dole out the worn coinage instead of paying out our own created values. The question is, Does the metal then still ring true or are our ideals no better than currency debased, or counterfeit? Ibsen, properly understood, finds our gold is still genuine. That gold is the truth within us, which must be dug up from under the rubbish of hypocrisy. We need to be regenerated from within. Without that, liberative measures, be they even revolutions, are of no avail.

Meanwhile, the world has become accustomed to compound with its conscience. Let us instance the *casus conscientiæ* in its widest occurrence. We talk as much as ever, and as glibly and sentimentally, about the saving grace of brotherly love; and after a fashion we do practice the commandment that we should love our neighbor. But will any self-respecting business man hold up his head and declare, of a week day and in business hours, that his

INDEX